Praise for *Inside the Minds*

"Need-to-read inside information and analysis that will improve your bottom line - the best source in the business." – Daniel J. Moore, Member, Harris Beach LLP

"The Inside the Minds series is a valuable probe into the thought, perspectives, and techniques of accomplished professionals..." – Chuck Birenbaum, Partner, Thelen Reid & Priest

"Aspatore has tapped into a gold mine of knowledge and expertise ignored by other publishing houses." – Jack Barsky, Managing Director, Information Technology & Chief Information Officer, ConEdison *Solutions*

"Unlike any other publisher – actual authors that are on the front-lines of what is happening in industry." – Paul A. Sellers, Executive Director, National Sales, Fleet and Remarketing, Hyundai Motor America

"A snapshot of everything you need..." – Charles Koob, Co-Head of Litigation Department, Simpson Thacher & Bartlet

"Everything good books should be - honest, informative, inspiring, and incredibly well-written." – Patti D. Hill, President, BlabberMouth PR

"Great information for both novices and experts." – Patrick Ennis, Partner, ARCH Venture Partners

"A rare peek behind the curtains and into the minds of the industry's best." – Brandon Baum, Partner, Cooley Godward

"Intensely personal, practical advice from seasoned dealmakers." – Mary Ann Jorgenson, Coordinator of Business Practice Area, Squire, Sanders & Dempsey

"Great practical advice and thoughtful insights." – Mark Gruhin, Partner, Schmeltzer, Aptaker & Shepard, PC

"Reading about real-world strategies from real working people beats the typical business book hands down." - Andrew Ceccon, Chief Marketing Officer, OnlineBenefits Inc.

"Books of this publisher are syntheses of actual experiences of real-life, hands-on, front-line leaders--no academic or theoretical nonsense here. Comprehensive, tightly organized, yet nonetheless motivational!" - Lac V. Tran, Sr. Vice President, CIO and Associate Dean Rush University Medical Center

"Aspatore is unlike other publishers...books feature cutting-edge information provided by top executives working on the front-line of an industry." - Debra Reisenthel, President and CEO, Novasys Medical Inc

www.Aspatore.com

Aspatore Books, a Thomson Reuters Business is the largest and most exclusive publisher of C-level executives (CEO, CFO, CTO, CMO, partner) from the world's most respected companies and law firms. Aspatore annually publishes a select group of C-level executives from the Global 1,000, top 250 law firms (partners and chairs), and other leading companies of all sizes. C-Level Business Intelligence™, as conceptualized and developed by Aspatore Books, provides professionals of all levels with proven business intelligence from industry insiders—direct and unfiltered insight from those who know it best—as opposed to third-party accounts offered by unknown authors and analysts. Aspatore Books is committed to publishing an innovative line of business and legal books, those which lay forth principles and offer insights that, when employed, can have a direct financial impact on the reader's business objectives, whatever they may be. In essence, Aspatore publishes critical tools—need-to-read as opposed to nice-to-read books—for all business professionals.

Inside the Minds

The critically acclaimed *Inside the Minds* series provides readers of all levels with proven business intelligence from C-level executives (CEO, CFO, CTO, CMO, partner) from the world's most respected companies. Each chapter is comparable to a white paper or essay and is a future-oriented look at where an industry/profession/topic is heading and the most important issues for future success. Each author has been carefully chosen through an exhaustive selection process by the *Inside the Minds* editorial board to write a chapter for this book. *Inside the Minds* was conceived in order to give readers actual insights into the leading minds of business executives worldwide. Because so few books or other publications are actually written by executives in industry, *Inside the Minds* presents an unprecedented look at various industries and professions never before available.

The Law School Librarian's Role as an Educator

Leading Librarians on Adapting to New Technologies, Maximizing Research Skills, and Helping Students Transition from Law School to Law Firm

ASPATORE

Mat #40753602

Inside the Minds Project Manager, Andrea Peterson; edited by Michaela Falls; proofread by Melanie Zimmerman

ISBN 978-0-314-19479-4

For corrections, updates, comments or any other inquiries please e-mail TLR.AspatoreEditorial@thomson.com.

First Printing, 2008
10 9 8 7 6 5 4 3 2 1

CONTENTS

Michelle Rigual   7
Associate Director and Assistant Professor of
Law Librarianship
University of New Mexico School of Law Library
TEACHING A NEW DOG THE SAME OLD TRICK

James E. Duggan   19
Associate Law Library Director and Professor
Southern Illinois University School of Law Library
MEETING THE NEEDS OF TOMORROW'S
LIBRARY USER TODAY

Joyce A. McCray Pearson   31
Director and Associate Professor of Law
The University of Kansas School of Law,
Wheat Law Library
THE DIRECTOR AND LAW SCHOOL LIBRARIAN'S
ROLE AS EDUCATOR

Janis L. Johnston   51
Director, Associate Professor of Law and
Associate Professor of Library Administration
Albert E. Jenner, Jr. Memorial Law Library, College of Law,
University of Illinois at Urbana-Champaign
CONSTANT MISSION: CHANGING METHODS

Darla Jackson   61
Head of Reference and Access Services
Oklahoma City University Law Library
TEACHING EFFECTIVE LEGAL RESEARCH

Christopher Simoni   77
Library Director and Professor of Law
Drexel University Earle Mack School of Law
TEACHING THE QUESTIONS, NOT THE ANSWERS

Darcy Kirk   85
*Associate Dean for Library and Technology
and Professor of Law*
University of Connecticut School of Law
*THE LAW SCHOOL LIBRARIAN: FILLING
IN THE GAPS*

Patrick Meyer   99
*Associate Library Director and
Adjunct Professor of Law*
Thomas Jefferson School of Law
*TRAINING THE NEXT GENERATION OF LAWYERS:
TEACHING ESSENTIAL RESEARCH SKILLS*

Barbara Bintliff   121
*Nicholas Rosenbaum Professor of Law and Director,
William A. Wise Law Library*
University of Colorado at Boulder
*THE ROLES AND STATUS OF THE ACADEMIC LAW
LIBRARY DIRECTOR*

Barbara Glennan   137
Assistant Director for Electronic and Outreach Services
California Western School of Law
*WORKING WITH STUDENTS AND FACULTY IN THE
RESEARCH PROCESS*

Appendices   149

Teaching a New Dog the Same Old Trick

Michelle Rigual

Associate Director and Assistant Professor
of Law Librarianship

University of New Mexico School of Law Library

ASPATORE

I have been involved in the management of law school libraries for five years, which has given me only a short-term perspective on how the role of a law school library is evolving. I haven't decided yet whether we are in the midst of faster than normal evolutionary processes or a genuine paradigm shift. But it is clear that rapid technological advances, rising material costs, and stagnant budgets require smart managers who are engaged in the important discussions in the field of law librarianship.

Library Management Goals

The mission of a law school library is shaped, in large part, by the law school's mission. The mission differs somewhat from school to school but generally includes educating and training students to become more than competent lawyers who will make a meaningful contribution to the legal community combined with harnessing the resources concentrated in the law school to bring about social improvement. The law school library assists the law school in meeting its mission. Its goals are created when it focuses the larger mission through the lens of library services and values and may be stated broadly as making efficient use of the state's or university's resources to acquire and manage legal information, educate and train students and attorneys, and create space for all of these activities.

Benchmarks to Measure Success

We have established benchmarks to measure success in the courses we teach, but it is much harder to measure success when you are just one piece of the larger picture. I have never encountered a law school library's claim of responsibility for some portion of the increase in bar passage rate, or other similar outcome-related measure. Law school libraries measure their success in terms of comparative statistics and user satisfaction.

Libraries compare their package of services and holdings with each other via the ABA's annual questionnaire that counts the number of titles, serial subscriptions, electronic licenses, interlibrary loan requests placed and filled, seats available, hours, circulations, and librarians, staff members and students who work at the library. Beyond the ABA and any other annual questionnaire requirements, a wise law school library manager counts everything they do and uses those numbers to their advantage whenever possible—in promotional material, funding requests, and prepared sound bites. It is always useful to be able to tell your dean that you doubled the number of faculty research requests filled.

The legal researcher measures the library's effectiveness by whether the library contains the materials needed to answer the legal research question; whether the materials were clearly up to date; whether the materials were easy to find; whether assistance was easily available if needed; and once found, whether it was easy to carry the information out of the library (e-mail, copy, print). Also, whether the researcher was relatively comfortable while engaged in the process (from parking to seating to desk space). Such feedback is important—every complaint, if taken seriously, is an opportunity to improve the library.

Key Services of Today's Law School Library

The key services of today's law school library are acquiring and managing legal information; educating and training legal researchers; and providing space that fosters studying, thinking, and intellectual interaction.

The process of legal information acquisition and management is complicated. It calls for understanding the materials that are critical to the law, long-range planning, keeping up with changes in technology, and finding the most economical means to provide the information. We decide what we need to have "just in case" and what we can have "just in time." Just in case materials are listed in the ABA standards and should always be at the ready just in case they are needed. For these materials, we decide what format they should be in, devise methods to facilitate access to them, and manage their upkeep. Just in time materials are outside the collection development policy but are needed to complete a patron's legal research. We know how to get these materials quickly. Even should all legal materials one day become digital, our role will be to understand them in their most current format, know how to transfer them into the next format, and to bridge the gap between formats.

Law school libraries also provide education and training programs. Law students and attorneys can no longer expect that formats will remain static. Certainly, we train people to use legal information in its current format but we also educate them in the more important lesson of understanding the sources and structure of the information as well as the typical ways it is stored and efficiently retrieved. These are skills that can be applied when the information is presented differently and will help users understand legal material as it transitions to its next format.

Of course, law school libraries also provide a space to study, think, and interact intellectually. Though this service sounds basic, it is one of the most highly valued by all of our various types of patrons.

Key Skills for Law Library Managers

The skill I am most frequently called on to use is change management. Though many librarians and staff members in libraries are change-averse and risk-averse, they are experiencing frequent changes to their daily tasks and they see that when people leave they are often not replaced but rather the opportunity is taken to streamline processes. Traditional and familiar print materials still take many people to manage and handle, but those materials represent a smaller and smaller portion of the acquisitions budget. Thus, the change-averse among us are living in a state of high stress, and sometimes outright fear; they recognize that the skills that served them well for many years are not as highly valued today.

The skills that are necessary for change management are strikingly similar to those needed for project management in general; they seem different because they involve so many more people and the effect on them is profound. The skills include the ability to motivate and train people to constantly improve; the ability to plan many steps into the future; the ability to set up a structure that gives people support; and the ability to communicate a vision and the specific steps required to get there. The most important attribute required is patience. It is not usually a disaster if a project fails; just pick up and start over with the lessons learned. Failure at change management threatens the stability that people rely upon.

The second key skill for law school library managers is the ability to simultaneously understand the big picture and detail. People who see only the big picture dump too much work on others, risk never allowing any project to be completed, and do not respect the work of those who wrestle with the details. Those who only see details cannot make the pieces work together. They waste precious resources chasing down the irrelevant, damaging the overall system. More than any other skill that I list, I think the ability to see both the big picture and the detail is an inherent quality. If someone has it, they get better at it by learning more about both the detail and the structure, and then through years of mid-level management where it is common to move back and forth between them.

The third key skill for law school library managers is the ability to identify opportunities for improvement, whether it be improved workflow for a department or partnering with another library to provide a better service. Ideally, improvement should not come in large changes, but in constant, incremental change. This minimizes stress for all employees and creates a culture of seeking to improve. Thus, the responsibility for improvement does not fall on any single person, but on all. The best source for obtaining this skill is to see it in practice, and to try to act on it. Facility with this skill is gained with practice. The ability to identify opportunities for improvement also requires self-reflection and strong communication skills.

Fourth, law school library managers should be able to create a system where work can be delegated and timely feedback provided. Organizational structure makes a huge difference. There has to be enough slack in the system that people can be shifted to where they are most needed and they need to know whether the work they are doing is of the type and quality expected. This skill is developed by closely observing different systems, knowing the resources available, using the organization's strengths, and working around or fixing its weaknesses.

Finally, law school library managers need the ability to set goals, steps for completion, and reasonable deadlines; identify resources needed for completion; and measure success. These skills distinguish proactive and reactive behavior. They couple thought and action, since neither is enough alone. They allow a project to be seen to completion rather left half done. Again, these skills are learned from seeing them done, practicing, and working through them with others.

Top Budget Items for Law School Libraries

Salaries are the number one budget items for most law school libraries, especially if the money budgeted for travel, recruitment, and professional service contracts (copier specialists, consultants, professional movers who can handle large-scale shifts) are added. After salaries and other personnel-related expenses, the order of the following budget items can vary, depending on the library's mix of materials and needs: electronic licenses, serial print materials, monographic print materials, and equipment and furniture.

Salaries and materials have always been the two largest budget items. This has not changed as materials have become available electronically; what has changed and continues to do so is the larger and larger percentage of the budget for which these electronic licenses account and the high inflation rate on supplementation for print serials, which for one vendor have been noted to have increased nearly 13 percent annually between 1995 to 2006. Equipment and furniture costs are also quite high as computers, projectors, high-quality phones and phone lines, document cameras, smart boards and interactive pens, archival and desktop scanners, and other technologies may come out of the library budget. Also, furniture needs change as equipment needs change.

It is the rare law school library budget that receives annual increases.

Job Titles and Staffing Models

The key job titles in a law school library generally include director; associate/assistant Director; head of public services; head of reference; head of technical services; head of access services; reference librarian; electronic resources librarian; collection development librarian; acquisitions librarian; systems librarian; cataloger; and circulation, serials, and acquisitions clerks. Few law school libraries can have all of these titles, but all of the functions need to be assigned. There are as many variations as there are libraries, but the variations tend to follow a few patterns.

The dividing line between director and associate/assistant director varies quite a bit from library to library. Most directors set and monitor the budget because this is the one area that can never be safely delegated except in cases where the law school of university library keeps tight control over the law school library budget. The director will always be held responsible for the money and any mismanagement of it. After that their roles vary widely based on such things as their level of experience, preference, the amount of scholarship they engage in, and the level of their involvement in law school or university-level library administrative work. Collection development and acquisitions positions often exist or not, depending on how much of these roles the director wants to fill.

It seems there are frequently both a head of public services and a head of reference. This is mirrored in technical services with both a head of technical services and numerous librarians with distinct technical services titles. The variation seems to have a great deal to do with the history of the library. In both cases, the size of the library is an important factor in how many levels of hierarchy are needed. It is not good to have as many people in management as are managed. People who are so heavily managed tend to end up with restrictive roles within their libraries, and become unproductive and bored.

Electronic resources librarians are growing in popularity. The person in this position tends to be in charge of all facets of all things electronic, and is not limited by the functional titles that define most library positions. Other libraries do not have someone who deals specifically with the electronic resources, but requires everyone to deal with the electronic material that falls within their area. In this structure, all reference librarians are expected to be well versed in using their library's electronic resources; the collection development librarian chooses print and electronic resources, and the technical services personnel treat them as any other resource to be ordered and cataloged, though the work process will differ after that point.

In many instances, these roles are merging, and it is becoming rare to find a librarian who has a single function. All of the positions require solid project management skills. Interestingly, many heads of technical services fear that their role is being phased out, but I believe that this is one of the most highly valuable roles in the library. It is certainly one of the hardest to fill.
I do not think that there is a single staffing model that is best, and I look at the staffing process as dynamic. It should be shaped by the law school's

needs, the library's needs and priorities, and the skills and talents of the librarians. If a library director is well integrated into the law school, the associate/assistant director will take over many of their duties. If not, the director will be more hands on. The best staffing models allow people the flexibility to grow and develop special interests and flexibility for project work to be delegated, and provide timely and meaningful feedback to employees. Librarians should have a variety of tasks, but not have to jump back and forth between widely divergent duties. There should not be more people managing than there are people who are managed and people should not have to go long periods without speaking to their supervisor.

Responding to Change

Many years of high inflation for library materials and stagnant budgets means that law school libraries have to make some changes. More realistically, it means that they have been making changes and will need to continue to do so. The most obvious way to lower costs is to look to the places the money is spent: staff and materials.

Before legal material was available electronically, libraries needed multiple copies of core items. Because that need no longer exists, elimination of duplication is an excellent place to start cutting costs. The next step is to eliminate the purchase of material in multiple formats because it is probably not necessary to own something in print, microform, and electronically. This step is more difficult than just canceling subscriptions to extra copies as it requires identifying what is held in the various formats and then deciding which format is most appropriate for that material and for the particular mix of patrons the library serves. Going further into the collection, another candidate for elimination is material by different authors that covers the same substance. Again, this is a difficult decision requiring a comparison of the author's depth and style of treatment, the type of use generally made by patrons, and the price of the various formats of the items. Once the decision has been made to keep a print subscription, the update schedule should be examined to decide whether all of the updates the publisher sends are actually needed. Perhaps the item can be put on a two, three, or four year rotation meaning that updates are not purchased but the whole set is replaced in the chosen number of years. The ability to do this depends on how quickly the law is changing in the subject area. The cost of labor should be included in calculations of the savings that will be realized from this update schedule. After eliminating duplication within a collection, a next step is to consider eliminating duplication between libraries. Some libraries have experimented with collaborative collection development to minimize costs.

Similarly, libraries need to identify and eliminate duplicative and wasteful work flow and processes within the library. The same theory should be applied outside the library, too. Rather than creating an infrastructure for processes it might be more efficient to tap the expertise of the law school or the university's other libraries and partner with them.

Another response to change is that law school libraries are trying to take better care of their materials. Library disaster planning and recovery knowledge has exploded since Hurricane Katrina. One of the lessons learned is that libraries need to look critically at their facilities to determine where they are vulnerable in case of fire, flood, or other disaster. Highly valuable materials should not be housed in these vulnerable spots. Another consideration is how to simplify recovery after a disaster. The job of recovery will be much easier if the most valuable items are near each other and easily distinguishable from other material.

Rapid advancements in digital technology have created new methods of performing old tasks, new expectations from patrons, and new capabilities for the law school library. The effects of these rapid advancements are not limited to the library. One recent Sunday, the *New York Times* front page carried a story that described the recent rebirth of haggling for relatively inexpensive consumer items. Customers now have so much comparative pricing and quality information available to them that they arrive at stores demanding that the price be lowered to meet what they can get across town or online. Across the page was a story about movie theaters becoming venues for high-quality (even 3D) showings of sporting events or Metropolitan Opera shows. The spread of digital technology to most theaters makes this service possible. Another push is the need to find new revenue due to movie audiences getting their movies on demand at home where they can watch them on a theater-sized high-definition television.

In the law school library new methods of performing old tasks appear every day. An obvious and simple example is ordering a book. This is almost exclusively done through vendor Web sites, whether Amazon or a library vendor such as YBP. Everyone is familiar with the ease and speed of this process. Returns and credits are generally simple and purchase and payment histories are often available. These Web sites can be seen as merely moving an old process from the mail or phone to the Internet, but they have also made it easy to complete a large number of different processes in one place. This reduces the need for specialization and blurs the dividing line between traditional job categories.

The example of purchasing a book is also useful for demonstrating the role of new expectations. As with the customers haggling over the price of Ralph Lauren pants or Canon cameras, library patrons' expectations have changed. A few short years ago, they might wait weeks to receive an item that they needed but that their library did not own. Everyone knows that Amazon will ship a book overnight and they expect that level of service. Library users also expect up-to-date equipment in the library and to be able to access digital information from remote locations. Unfortunately, they also expect all of this to happen without new funds.

Digitization of rare materials and special collection items is the library world's version of a movie theater's 3D showing of the Metropolitan Opera, though not as flashy. As funds become scarce, many libraries look critically at their collections hoping to find items that can be canceled. In doing so, they sometimes find unexpected gems. In the past, if a library wanted to protect an item it put it away in a rare book room or closed archive where it was safe but inaccessible. Digitization allows an alternative and is another example of the fact that, despite rapid change, the goals of law school libraries remain essentially simple in nature and unchanged.

As associate director of the University of New Mexico Law Library, Michelle Rigual has responsibility for the library's day-to-day operations, overseeing faculty and public services, technical services, electronic resources, and collection development. She teaches advanced legal research, specialized legal research, and critical thinking. Additionally, she works closely with the administrative staff on personnel and facilities issues and fiscal matters.

Ms. Rigual joined the law library faculty in February 2003 as a reference librarian. She has since served as co-interim director; head of technical services; and assistant director for technical services, electronic resources, and collections. Before coming to UNM, she worked as a reference librarian at Arizona State University Law Library and Capital University Law Library. Prior to her library work, she spent four years with the Army Corps of Engineers Construction Engineering Research Laboratory, where she wrote compliance assessment manuals and conducted environmental assessments of military installations in the United States, Italy, and Turkey.

Ms. Rigual received her B.A. from the University of Texas and her J.D. and M.S. from the University of Illinois.

Dedication: *To Sheldon, Jenn, Mom, and Dad*

Meeting the Needs of Tomorrow's Library User Today

James E. Duggan

Associate Law Library Director and Professor

Southern Illinois University School of Law Library

ASPATORE

Thoughts on Leadership

A number of issues make managing a law school library in today's environment more challenging than it was five years ago. The budget of a typical academic law library has not increased along with inflation or the rising publisher prices for needed legal resources (either in print or online). In most cases, because of inflation, library managers have had to cut long-standing print titles, or scale back electronic subscriptions in order to make sure there is enough money to balance the budget. In addition, skyrocketing costs of serials and practitioner loose-leaf sets have prevented libraries from establishing comprehensive collections in some subject areas.

Although some law libraries may not be seeing as much in-house usage as they had previously, users are demanding more and more electronic access to library materials from their computer desktops. Consequently, library staffing has been changing to provide workers with more familiarity with electronic issues, including electronic contract and license negotiation (such as agreeing on simultaneous user limits, procuring library-wide access using Internet protocol (IP) addresses vs. user passwords, and knowing when to agree to non-disclosure contractual clauses); information technology troubleshooting; and increased user instruction.

A need to balance print resources with electronic materials also makes law library management a challenge. Although younger users demand electronic access, a notable cadre of older users (including some law school faculty) remain unconvinced that electronic access is a better option than print resources.

Measuring the Library's Effectiveness for Researchers

The modern legal researcher expects the academic law library to provide ready access to legal materials, either in electronic format or print, and to make that access easily available. If the law library does not have the particular source, then the researcher typically expects the law library to quickly obtain access though cooperative electronic agreements with the main university; other databases; or through the efficient use of interlibrary loan. Today's user also expects nearly seamless interaction with the library via its Web site or online catalog. If visiting the library in person, the researcher expects quick, friendly service from knowledgeable staff.

If the researcher does not receive the expected service, then various feedback mechanisms need to be employed to ensure that the library learns of the researcher's lack of satisfaction, and more importantly, acts on the feedback provided. Such feedback mechanisms include virtual "suggestion" boxes; occasional online surveys; or most importantly, well-publicized e-mail or print contact information for the law library management, in which the researcher can easily express concerns and questions in a painless and easily accomplished manner.

The feedback provided must be properly acknowledged; acted upon if appropriate; and shared with all affected staffing areas to ensure that staff members are aware of possible concerns. The law library can only attempt to improve its programs and services if it is aware of user concerns and problems.

Evaluating and Preparing for New Technologies

Each law school library evaluates technology differently, depending on the proposed usage and benefit to the library patron base. For example, a complex online public access catalog is viewed in a different manner than a standalone database, because the online catalog is generally the user's first portal to the library's collection, and may control access to circulation, serials records, reserves, and other library services, whereas a standalone database typically has one set of user instructions and guides that do not interact with other library database access points. Although cost is a major criterion, it is not always the deciding factor, and may be considered in connection with a number of other characteristics, including ease of use; integration with other systems and programs; ability to access outside of law school and law library firewalls; availability of usage statistics; user response; and availability of training materials.

Vendors who have a good reputation generally benefit from quick adoption of new products by law libraries, while new companies may have a steeper curve in convincing libraries to try their products, unless the new technology meets a need not met by prior products in the field (for example, the introduction of Hein-on-Line in 2000 met an unmet need of providing electronic access to law review articles in PDF format; previously law review articles were available in html or other electronic format only through LexisNexis, Westlaw, or the law review's Web site). A "good reputation" is determined by the quality of the product; how responsive the vendor is to questions and concerns raised by the library; availability of training guides and other materials used to promote the product; and overall perceived value provided. Librarians who express a preference for a particular vendor's product typically need to explain why such a preference exists, and demonstrate how additional products from this vendor will benefit library users and the overall library program of services. For example, Hein recently added popular a la carte collections such as *U.S. Congressional Documents* and *Foreign and International Law Resources Database* to its popular Hein-on-Line service. Knowing the quality and ease of use of the basic Hein-on-Line service made the positive decision to add these additional databases fairly easy for many librarians.

The most important step a law library can take in order to be prepared for new technologies is not to lock into a specific library system or database that cannot be upgraded or integrated with forthcoming technology advances. Especially troublesome are stand-alone programs or systems that fail to interact with other programs, including standard operating systems such as Windows or Linux. For example, if your library is using a stand-alone cataloging system that does not interact with your circulation system, then patrons would typically not be able to request interlibrary loans or check the status of reserve items. Law librarians should demand interactive systems whenever possible.

Librarians, especially those charged with responsibility for computer services, instructional technologies or systems should also monitor trends in legal technologies, and keep management apprised of new hardware and software features. Examples of newer technologies currently affecting law libraries include self-checkout hardware, Radio Frequency Identification (RFID), Library 2.0 standards, and Functional Requirements for Bibliographic Records (FRBR). New technologies can also be learned about at tradeshow exhibits and meetings, as well as vendor presentations and sponsorships.

Librarians should approach emerging technologies with a "practiced eye," and carefully evaluate how the new technology might fit into the overall library and law school picture. The pace of technological change has increased in the past twenty years, and "early adopter" libraries sometimes find that they may have jumped too soon. For example, compact disc (CD) towers were embraced by many libraries at a time when the technology was quickly moving toward online database subscriptions. While the CD-ROM technology was heavily utilized by the legal profession, the technology's limitations (e.g., need for networking towers, CD-ROM passwords and expiration dates, necessity for individual loading of CD-ROMs, etc.) made adoption by law school libraries problematic, and it was ultimately rejected as newer formats such as DVDs and Internet-based electronic databases quickly became popular.

As more and more library patrons prefer electronic access to library resources, librarians need to balance the overall cost of new technology to the benefits conferred by the technology. Among the possible benefits include increased access; less processing costs (especially if a corresponding print title can be cancelled); additional searching and indexing options; and a greater electronic reputation for the law library. Legal researchers can benefit from being able to access newer systems via the library's catalog or Web site, or use databases that were developed as part of a university system-wide arrangement.

Top Budget Items for Law School Libraries

Personnel, library materials, database and other electronic subscriptions, equipment, and supplies make up the largest portions of an academic law library budget, with salaries and other staffing costs comprising the lion's share. Although library staffs have grown in size over the past thirty years, the biggest growth has been in the cost of library materials and database/electronic subscriptions. These costs are expected to continue to rise as legal publishers consolidate and revise their revenue model.

One of the current favored financial techniques used to manage the law library budget is a careful accounting of all monies expended in the past year, which is used to predict how much will be spent in subsequent years. These statistics are then used to determine what resources (especially serials) the library can afford. For example, a library may only buy a supplement or pocket-part set every other year (to update a resource), or in more extreme cases, it may decide to buy an updated title every couple of years.

Another management technique offered by at least one publisher is to enter into a library materials agreement with the library, wherein the library agrees to purchase certain library materials on a multi-year basis, and the publisher agrees to limit cost increases to a discounted percentage. Libraries that have entered into such agreements agree not to cancel publisher titles during the life of the contract, except at certain specified intervals. Many libraries have adopted this method as a way to contain certain regular costs and provide some predictability in the budgeting process.

Libraries that invest in computer equipment have been traditionally placing equipment replacement on a three or four year cycle, thus spreading expensive computer replacement costs over a longer period of time.

For a typical law library budget, personnel salaries usually form the biggest chunk of the regular budget, with library resources spending ranging from 20 to 40 percent. The larger the budget percentage spent on library materials, the better, as the library is generally judged by patrons and other users by the size, scope, and updated nature of its collection. Although larger law school libraries may have more resources devoted to the collection, they typically have more staff in order to purchase, process, and make new materials available to library patrons.

Unfortunately, in recent years the rising cost of legal materials (which has often outpaced inflation) has meant that law library budgets have not been as robust as they have been in past years; and library managers have often been forced to make cuts in either personnel or the collection (or both). One of the biggest challenges facing library managers today is ensuring collection strengths and library services while working with stagnant or reduced library budgets.

Review and approval of the library budget is usually done by the library director, with input from midlevel library managers. The dean of the law school typically decides on the amount available for allocation to the law library budget.

ROI Calculations

Academic law libraries are not typically profit centers (neither, typically, are law schools); however, the continued growth in the cost of legal resources means that law libraries must be extremely cost efficient when expending monies from the budget. A savvy law library manager should look at all cost centers—from personnel, supplies, and equipment to books and database subscriptions—and continually evaluate whether additions or cuts can be made, based on patron needs and economic demands. Although every library is different, basic services and collection needs (e.g., circulation, interlibrary loan, reference, cataloging, etc.) should typically be allocated the most in terms of scarce budget resources; while other programs and service add-ons (for example, access to high-cost but little-used databases, or buying library system enhancements that may not be worth the cost, i.e., adding photos to individual library patron records, etc.) may need to be cut, especially in times of economic downturns.

The library manager must also be in tune with current administration management objectives and goals in order to align the law library with the rest of the law school and larger university. For example, law schools that pride themselves on excellent student services face criticism if the law library is not on board with similar service levels. In addition, universities expect their college entities to be "good academic citizens" and law libraries are generally expected to collaborate with other campus libraries (especially in terms of collection development, service hours, and shared database acquisitions). A law library that is consistently highly rated by patrons (especially faculty and students) has a better chance of seeing its budget remain strong.

Helpful Associations and Alliances

As the premier worldwide law library association, the American Association of Law Libraries (AALL) offers a host of educational programming and networking opportunities for managers of law libraries. The AALL Annual Meeting presents nearly seventy educational programs on subjects germane to law libraries each year, many on management and offered at an intermediate or advanced level. In addition, AALL chapters provide educational opportunities at a local or regional level. Besides its annual meeting, AALL provides networking possibilities through its special interest sections (SISs), including an academic SIS, as well as other types of library or subject specific sections. AALL members can avail themselves of committee or SIS listservs, or sponsored online discussion groups on various subjects (e.g., recent offerings have included copyright, Web 2.0, and faculty services). Individual membership currently costs approximately $220 per year with SIS membership fees running $18 each. Annual meeting registration fees typically range from $400 to $515.

Law library directors also participate in the American Association of Law Schools, which offers training and other educational programming through its section on libraries, and other education events and workshops throughout the year. Institutional membership in AALS is typically paid by the law school. Regional AALS sections are also a possibility.

Other alliances that are helpful to law library management include consortiums, e.g., the New England Law Library Consortium (NELLCO) and the Mid America Law Library Consortium (MALLCO), which assist libraries in purchasing group-wide database subscriptions and equipment additions (membership costs vary by group); the Center for Computer-Assisted Legal Instruction (CALI), which provides more than 600 interactive lessons on law and law-related subjects as well as ongoing technology projects for law school use (law school membership costs vary); and local bar association groups (whose members can provide input on how local patrons use the law library).

Auditing Law School Library Services and Resources

Assuming accreditation by the American Bar Association and Association of American Law Schools, the sabbatical site inspection every seven years is an excellent way to make sure library services and resources are on par with law school expectations and other law school libraries of similar size and purpose. The site inspection, which is typically preceded by the formation of an internal self-study committee and report, offers a regular way to audit law library programs and make sure that the mission and goals of the library are being met (in conjunction with the law school).

Outside of the sabbatical inspection, the law library can use both external and internal processes to ensure that user needs are being met and library services and resources are appropriate. Among the outside processes are regular use of a library committee, which functions as a sounding board for potential purchases or changes in library programmatic features. Regular interaction with law school faculty also helps to gauge satisfaction levels, as do requests for faculty input on collection deficiencies or new areas of concentration. Library staff members are also important contributors to determining how library services are faring, and should be frequently consulted.

Meeting Expectations

Most users expect that the law library will provide ready access to the materials needed for research; helpful staff who will provide guidance and research assistance; and a comfortable and welcoming environment. Law faculty members expect an up-to-date resource center that owns the materials they need, or that can provide quick access through electronic means or interlibrary loan. Faculty members also expect the library staff to provide efficient and knowledgeable reference; contribute bibliographies and other resource guides; and organize and maintain the collection in a responsible manner.

Students may have similar but occasionally different expectations, including full electronic access to both legal and non-legal sources; fully accessible course reserves; integration with other campus library resources; and home access to most (if not all) library resources. Depending on the facility, students may also see the library as a quiet place to study or just "hang out," as well as a place where librarians and other staff can provide advice on research projects. Libraries can attract student usage by employing approachable and service-oriented staff and enacting student-friendly policies (such as allowing some food and drink in the facilities; designating quiet areas; and reduced or rescinded student circulation fines). Libraries can also attract students by acquiring specific student-oriented materials, including study guides; extra copies of class textbooks; and non-legal materials (for example, several academic law libraries hold extensive popular movie collections on DVD for patron use).

Of these various expectations, the hardest to meet is ensuring that the library has the right mix of print and electronic resources. Although there is a growing preference for electronic sources, not everything is available in a digital format, and patrons hoping that they will never have to come into the library may occasionally be disappointed, especially when looking for historic or out-of print resources, such as early statutes or treatises. In addition, a significant segment of the library user population still prefers materials in print, or lacks proper training about how to find sources online. Libraries must continue to provide bibliographic training for their users, whether in person or online through frequently asked questions files (FAQs) and research guides.

How do libraries gauge user satisfaction? Obviously, user surveys are the traditional answer, whether done in writing or via electronic means such as e-mail or Web-based questionnaires. However, other systems are being developed to help evaluate how patrons are using and benefiting from library services. For example, use statistics are now being provided for electronic database use (including full-text case law and periodical sources), and online public access catalogs provide both statistics and actual searches to enable library staff to judge how effectively the online catalog is being used. The library should provide some sort of evaluative instrument for any new service that is offered, and should periodically survey users about traditional programs and assistance being offered. Libraries that fail to ask users about what is working (and what is not) will find that they are no longer relevant to the law school enterprise, and will ultimately lose their purpose (as well as funding).

Final Thoughts

Being a successful manger of a law school library suggests that you have learned how to be flexible, even while observing several core values. Academic law libraries have changed a great deal over the past thirty years, with more changes to come as we continue to face increased costs for both print and electronic resources; an evolving law faculty and student body that expect instantaneous electronic access; and law school administrations that expect libraries to do more with less.

As libraries have progressed from print repositories to hybrid electronic storehouses, a manager must progress as well, and be able to identify trends and opportunities that enable the law library to continue to serve basic needs and expectations, as well as offer new programs and services. Academic libraries must stay ahead of the curve, and prepare law students for using the databases and resources that they will encounter in the practice world. Merely building a standard collection today will not suffice for tomorrow's attorney, and a library manager must continue to refine the library's mission and goals to accurately reflect the future objectives and needs of the legal profession.

Even if the librarian has not been absolutely correct in terms of predicting what the future holds, being flexible will help in dealing with the challenges that the library faces, especially if you can be nimble while moving around resources and personnel to meet unmet needs. This flexibility also allows you to deal with the vagaries of a constantly changing administration, who may suggest different priorities depending on the makeup of the library committee, or the incumbent in the dean's office. Knowledge of this flexibility will help your staff learn how to interact with you, as it suggests that management decisions may change over time as new trends and programs come to light. A manager who stubbornly clings to a library service long after the need for it has disappeared will soon find that he or she will be dealing with a disgruntled library staff and a suspicious administration.

The librarian's ultimate goal is to continue to provide a collection that is either being used by the library's primary patrons, or will be used in the future. A flexible library manager will not abandon this core value, even in the face of stagnant or decreasing budgets; naysayers who suggest the library's days are numbered; and/or users who question every acquisition. Library managers must continuously "make the case" for the library's place in the law school hierarchy, and consistently demonstrate the necessary role of the library for law faculty and students; other university students and personnel; and the general public.

James E. Duggan will become law library director and associate professor of law at Tulane University Law School, New Orleans, on July 1, 2008. From 1988 to 2008 he held several positions at Southern Illinois University School of Law Library, most recently as associate director and professor. He will serve as president of the American Association of Law Libraries (AALL) in 2008-09. Professor Duggan holds a B.A. from Virginia Tech, a J.D. from the University of Mississippi School of Law, and an M.L.I.S. from Louisiana State University.

The Director and Law School Librarian's Role as Educator

Joyce A. McCray Pearson

Director and Associate Professor of Law
The University of Kansas School of Law
Wheat Law Library

ASPATORE

Brief Information about the Author's Path to Law Librarianship

I went to law school after working for several years as a vocal music teacher, and while I was in law school, I spent a lot of time in the library doing research. I enjoyed my legal research class, which many students do not. During my second semester of law school I decided to work in the library as a student assistant; I had often contemplated going into librarianship, and when I worked in the library, I felt at home. It made law school make sense. I felt like I had found my "calling." I was told by the associate director that I would need a library degree to eventually apply for a director's position and I went ahead and pursued it, because I knew that this was the right career for me—primarily because I get to do so many different things, yet the hours are regular, and the stress is very manageable.

I attended the law librarianship program at the University of Washington in Seattle. It is ranked the number one program in law librarianship. It has a special librarianship program for people entering with law degrees. I took my first professional job at the University of Louisville Law School Library. Originally, I was a collection services and government documents librarian and then I became a reference international law librarian. I worked there for four years. I later accepted an electronic services librarian position at the University of Kansas School of Law Library and I was able to become the associate director after less than two years because of staff retirements and my educational background and experience. Today, I am the director of the school's law library.

The Unique Role of the Law School Librarian

A law school librarian's role largely depends on the structure of both the university and the law school where they work. For example, there are a number of law schools where librarians do not have tenure, and there are some law schools where the law library is autonomous from the university library system, and the philosophical mindset behind such factors is what directs the role of librarians in a law school. Librarians in a law school that does not have tenure track status may or may not be viewed somewhat differently from librarians at schools where there is tenure track. In many cases, when librarians are up for tenure and the law faculty on the promotion and tenure committee examines their promotion and tenure dossiers and files, they are very impressed and surprised to learn about the many different things that law librarians do in terms of the types of articles we write; the types of services we perform; and the types of teaching that we do. Librarians with tenure track status play an important role in the process of a law school education. That is not to say, by any means, that non-tenure track librarians do not teach and are not just as vital to legal education. The tenure track versus non-tenure track status issue is case specific to each institution. It is completely up to an individual whether they take a position at a school that requires tenure for librarians. Librarians who are on tenure track have requirements of professional performance and/or teaching, service to the law school, university community, and the profession, and scholarship. According to a recent survey, the Academic Law Librarian Tenure and Employment Statues Survey, www.aallnet.org/sis/allsiscst/index.html, only 23.3 percent of the law schools responding to the survey have tenure-track status for non-director librarians. Faculty status or tenure track for librarians is no longer the trend. Some universities and colleges have maintained the status historically, because they see no reason to do away with it and find that it works quite well in their institutions. Librarians with tenure enjoy academic freedom similar to that of other faculty and have an expectation of employment security. If the university values this and has historically maintained this philosophy it is quite possible that it will remain.

The lack of tenure status does not necessarily change the role of a librarian and the way they are perceived within the institution. Tenure status, however, adds to the duties and changes the focus of a librarian's day-to-day activities. The added stress of researching and writing, meeting publication deadlines, in addition to reference work, and administrative tasks make the status a lot less attractive to some who find it difficult to juggle a large number of tasks. Others enjoy the variety it adds to their work experience, and particularly those who need the rigor and the challenge of scholarship. It is not for everyone. There are many librarians, who are completely satisfied with their work, who do not engage in scholarly activities. And there are just as many law librarians who are not on tenure track who do engage in scholarly activities and teaching as those who are tenured or on tenure track. Therein lays the beauty of the profession. The important thing is for law librarians to find the right fit and the right place to engage in and have the experiences they need to feel successful and fulfilled.

"Tenure is the strongest protector of academic freedom. Tenure is a form of employment security in which an employee—a faculty member—is given an indefinite term of appointment in return for meeting certain qualifying criteria and specified continuing performance requirements…. Academic freedom and tenure go hand in hand in fulfilling a university's mission to create and disseminate new knowledge. Barbara A. Bintliff, Laura N. Gasaway, et.al, Rebuilding the Profession: Recommendations for Librarians Interested in Becoming Academic Law Library Directors, 99 *Law Libr. J.* 110 (2007).

I have often found that the way in which librarians are perceived within the law school and the way we perceive ourselves are rather different. We see ourselves as highly educated, skilled, and motivated people who are essential to the law school. But the truth of the matter is that some faculty and other people in the law school do not really understand what we do. Law librarians believe that a law library is the heart of the law school because it is where the research is done, and fortunately, we often find that as students begin to understand that all the information they need is not available on the Internet, they increasingly rely on law librarians for research and reference assistance. We are the stewards of the intellectual commons of the law school community.

It is really up to us to market ourselves as essential players in a law school. This can sometimes be difficult, because outside of a law school setting, librarians are typically viewed as generalists, similar to those who work in a public library. The reality is that law librarians, like librarians in all special libraries, are very different. Law library staffs with autonomous status from the university library system have to report to the dean of the law school and often librarians who have dual degrees—a J.D. and an M.L.S.—usually teach. Therefore, we feel that a law librarian's role is very different from that of librarians at a main university library, who are either bibliographers or professionals who service the university in a less intimate way. A law librarian's role is much more focused. Indeed, some of the main university libraries have hundreds of librarians, while there are often smaller staffs of librarians and staff members in law libraries who provide services for the law school and its faculty and students. We cannot really compare ourselves to anyone outside of our discipline. But that is okay because we like being special.

The Librarian's Relationship with Faculty

Law library directors are often viewed as just another faculty member. They attend faculty meetings and have a faculty vote; they hold tenure status at the university and teach various courses. However, we also handle a great deal of administrative work because numerous people report to us, a responsibility which other faculty members do not have. Similarly, other faculty members do not manage an extremely large budget. Therefore, we have a hybrid role; we view ourselves as members of the faculty who work both in the library and in the law school.

As law school librarians, we are in the business of serving our faculty; serving others in the school; serving the university; and serving students. Our staffs need to assist anyone who comes into the library or to the reference desk to find what they need. Most directors encourage law librarians to view themselves as people with faculty status who serve other faculty members as constituents; and to encourage lots of feedback from faculty.

One of a library's most important programs could be a library liaison program, called in some institutions a primary library contact service. Each librarian is assigned to six to ten faculty members, and assists them with their research and library needs. This type of service and program is very beneficial, because the librarians become experts in the faculty members' areas of research, and it creates a strong relationship between librarians and faculty members. Many law libraries have these programs.

Often, faculty members do not understand what librarians do, but by instituting a liaison program, they learn to understand that librarians can provide a variety of services, from compiling bibliographies to finding books; providing interlibrary loan (ILL) services; or conducting research in print or on the Web. Through a liaison program faculty members gain a deeper understanding of the talents of librarians and come to value how truly skilled and intellectual librarians are.

Primary Skills of a Library Director

A library director has to be an astute administrator and a member of the law faculty. A majority of academic law library director positions are faculty appointments. Id. Bintliff, at 102. As director you are responsible for the whole "kit and caboodle." There is generally a hierarchical level of administration and duties where all the librarians and staff members ultimately report, though sometimes not directly, to you. For example, ten students may report to the circulation manager and the circulation manger in turn reports to the library's head of public services who reports to the director. Other departments in the library are similarly situated. But long story short, "…an academic law library director is running a multimillion-dollar, not for-profit service organization. …. law libraries are pretty sizeable businesses that require solid administrative abilities as well as the talents that are necessary for achievement in an academic environment." Id. At 104.

A law library director wears a number of hats; in addition to managing staff, we conduct surveys, teach and assist students, and deal with a colossal amount of paperwork. Therefore, you have to be both flexible and focused in this role. We also act as adviser to our librarians who run the library on a day-to-day basis. We act as adviser to deans and associate deans routinely, as well as when emergencies at the university occur. We make snap decisions in these cases where we may have to schedule opening and closing the library at a different time. The trick to this is informing your constituents and students when sudden changes are made. Academic libraries are open for extraordinarily long hours, and even after the law school people have left for the day, the library is still open—and its staff members still have many responsibilities and liabilities. Libraries are open on weekends and at night, and all of those hours have to be covered by someone. And although directors often do not cover the service points in the library, they are ultimately responsible for every little positive or negative occurrence one could imagine could come up in an institution open to the public.

We meet these challenges by hiring and promoting people with experience and with proven abilities and skills in scheduling and serving in public service activities. And because resources are often limited, it takes a fair amount of creativity and much flexibility to make sure all the service points are covered with people who are qualified to deliver high-quality public service to all patrons.

There are three main skills law library directors must hone: management of the library's operations, involvement in the law school proper, and managing one's personal life. In addition there are three skills within those areas that must be attended to: the management of personnel, the libraries' resources and budget, and the strategic use of it and leadership. Leaders are forward thinkers and long range, and short-range planning is essential to the smooth running of an academic law library. Id. At 104 – 105.

The challenges lie in the constant balancing act of numerous competing, conflicting, and compatible interests including the different needs of students, patrons, and faculty, the different formats of materials, electronic vs. print, space issues, and other choices that must be made with limited resources.

The Law Library Director's Role as Educator—Teaching Law Students

The law library director's role as educator has two sides that often work well together but also often conflict. Id.at 106. The difficulty is in finding the balance between teaching, scholarly pursuits, and service activities as a faculty member and the successful oversight of the library and technology functions and other director administrative responsibilities. Teaching law students is an arduous task at best and it requires numerous hours of preparation for class lectures, and an inordinate amount of time to teach, grade, advise, and engage those curious young intellectual minds whose ultimate goal is to become the next great lawyer. Some of the students are a joy, while others are not. But overall, future lawyers are some of the most intelligent, young, old, and in-between people you will ever encounter.

One of the most important reasons to teach is that "…you truly become a faculty member and colleague of the other faculty members. The same classroom issues that matter to faculty also matter to you. Teaching establishes an area in which you can bond with your faculty colleagues, since curricular issues will take on the same personal dimension for you as it does for them. These strong bonds also deepen the faculty's overall trust in the director in his or her management role." Id. At 117.

Library directors teach a variety of courses. Often they teach the legal research component of first year law students' legal research and writing course. This course is often followed by an advanced legal research course that is also taught by directors or law librarians. In a survey that asked directors what they taught, 47 percent taught legal research, 21 percent taught advanced legal research, and 35 percent taught substantive or doctrinal courses. The courses include the following: admiralty, agency American Indian Law, animal law, business law, copyright, criminal procedure, cyberlaw, health law, intellectual property, law and literature, law library administration, property, torts, trademarks, wills and trust. For a complete list of courses see, Carol Bredemeyer, What Do Directors Do? 96 *Law Libr. J.* 317 (2004).

Teaching Future Librarians

There is another group of people law librarians must be committed to educating. Those people are our future law librarians. With the continual graying of our profession, it is essential that we educate and train tomorrow's law librarians. Over the next ten years, the baby boomer librarians will have to retire. This will create an obvious need for new librarians. James Milles, *Law Librarians as Educators and Role Models*, *The University at Buffalo's JD/MLS Program in Law Librarianship*, AALL Spectrum, July 2004, at pg. 20. Several ALA accredited library programs offer courses in law librarianship. A handful of law schools offer J.D./M.L.S. programs—Brooklyn Law School and Pratt Institute School of Information and Library Science, Indiana University, North Carolina Central University, Syracuse University, University at Buffalo, The State University of New York, University of Connecticut School of Law and Southern Connecticut State University Department of Library and Information Science, University of Iowa and Widener University School of Law and Clarion University of Pennsylvania. For a current list of all of the U.S. library schools, visit the Web site of the Conference of Law Library Educators (COLLE) at http://lib.law.washington.edu/colle/.

Recruiting qualified people into the profession is quite challenging. We are well aware of the great need to replace those who will soon be leaving the profession. It is important for directors and law librarians to encourage and develop relationships with students, lawyers, and others who we feel will enjoy and contribute to the law librarian community. The profession is not for everyone. As lawyers evolve in their legal work experience they learn that they may enjoy doing research and writing about legal resources and materials more than they care to interview clients, litigate, and attempt to resolve disputes. For these types of people law librarianship may appear to be the perfect place to utilize their special skills.

Law students who after one or two semesters of law school find a reference librarian or circulation manager particularly helpful and engaging may find themselves interested in becoming law librarians. It is up to us to foster these relationships and help develop future law librarians. We can form relationships and guide students, or lawyers, into our profession before the education requirements for the career are met. Many of us spend a considerable amount of our time discussing our job duties, job satisfaction, and career path with a number of second and third year law students. We must also be proactive with those who demonstrate an interest in law librarianship by guiding them to professional Web sites and sharing our profession directories and handbooks and other literature to help guide them or assist them in making a decision about their future in law librarianship.

Developing Good Research Skills: Best Practices

I believe that you cannot become a good researcher by simply reading a book about research or performing all your research electronically or on the Internet. It is imperative that people actually come into the library and actually do it. This is true even though so much research is done using proprietary databases, electronic resources, and the Internet. One of your first interactions with legal research is perhaps best performed in the law library with print materials. The print materials prepare you to perform good electronic legal research.

Typically, directors and law librarians teach a legal research class. Librarians generally handle reference services, and they teach law students on a one on one basis how to use the library catalog and other sources in the library, whether they are in print or online. These services are provided on a day-today basis as students come into the library with specific research needs. However, at our law school almost all of our librarians, whether they have M.L.S. or J.D. degrees, are very involved in the first year legal research and writing course, also called "lawyering" or "lawyering skills" courses. Librarians and reference staff, depending upon the institution, oftentimes teach small sections of approximately twenty first-year-law students. The students are given legal research exercises that they work on in the library, as well as instructional tours of the library materials. Students receive constant feedback from the librarian throughout these exercises; and as they are going through the research exercises in the library, they know that they can walk up to the reference desk to ask for help at any time.

At the next level, dual degree J.D./M.L.S. librarians give formal classroom lectures on advanced legal research, or they teach other classes in the curriculum such as law in popular culture or specialized legal research topics. Students who gravitate toward those specialized classes tend to like legal research and may want to go into a special topical area in their law practice. These tend to be smaller classes, where students are generally given some short assignments and then a final paper.

One of the most important best practices in teaching legal research skills is including feedback. Students are "feedback hungry" in law school, which is why it is a good idea to implement small sections for first year research classes that provide more one-on-one contact between student and librarian.

It is also important to teach students research skills that are relevant to today's law practice. Some of the courses include a comparative analysis of what types of research resources can be found in print and online, and how they are related to the actual practice of law. It is important for them to understand billing and the different ways to search databases at little or no cost. Simply put, we try to make the research process relevant to what the students are going to be doing when they get out of law school. A lot of the subject matter that you learn in law school is very theoretical, and students always want to know how they are going to use what they have learned when they go out into the real world. Librarians are skilled at showing students how they can use research sources that are free, or how to do research in the proprietary databases, LexisNexis and Westlaw, in such a way that you don't rack up a huge database charge and then have to overcharge their client.

Here are some of the best strategies in a nutshell:

1. Consult with law librarians early and often in the research process. It is especially important to determine whether Westlaw and/or LexisNexis billing is transactional or hourly, because many search strategies will depend upon the billing method. Also, take advantage of the toll-free customer support options offered by Westlaw (West Support Reference Attorneys) and LexisNexis (LexisNexis Live Research Help).

2. Take time to develop a search strategy that precisely frames the legal issues you are researching. This includes the crucial step of consulting secondary sources to discover relevant doctrine and terms of art.

3. Use print resources and free online sources to gather as much cheap information as possible before turning to the expensive Westlaw and LexisNexis databases. Do a cost/benefit analysis of price vs. efficiency to determine how much time each resource merits.

4. Look at the Westlaw (http://westlaw.com) LexisNexis (www.lexisnexis.com) directories and related information for free.

5. Use the "FOCUS" (LexisNexis) or "Locate" (Westlaw) features to narrow a search without typically accruing additional charges (for transactional billing).

6. Print from the browser using an attached printer to avoid print charges.

7. Familiarize yourself with the search protocols for "terms and connectors" searching to ensure your search accomplishes the intended goal and avoid duplicative searching.

8. Remember to sign off, especially if the billing is hourly. Otherwise, your account may be unnecessarily logged onto the server for a while.

There are some law students who simply cannot grasp the research experience, at first, and it is often because they come into law school with different skill sets or misinformation. In such cases, you have to back up and teach those students how to use a library, and how to perform analysis. Unfortunately, there is often a resistance and unwillingness on the part of many students to do the amount of digging that the research process entails; some of these students are somewhat undisciplined and do not appreciate the value of expending effort in the research process. In such cases, it often takes a small amount of failure on the part of the law students to realize that they need to work harder on their research skills; at that point, you need to take the time to work with the student on a one-on-one basis and let them see that there are many answers and variables in the research process. Research is not the kind of subject where you just fill in the blanks; there is a lot of work entailed, and sometimes you will miss the mark and have to start over again. That concept can be daunting for some students.

The Role of Technology in Educating Law Students

Technology is playing an increasingly significant role in the research process. Problems often arise when students believe that all of the information they need is online. This mistaken belief probably stems from the fact that today's students are very computer savvy; they take exams using laptops, they are addicted to e-mail and instant messaging. Unfortunately, laptops can be a distraction for students who think that they can surf the Internet and play solitaire while they are in class. Computer use has been very beneficial in the examination process because it often helps students to better organize their thoughts. It allows them to formulate ideas and gives them a similar experience to their computerized note taking tasks in class. Some students type faster than they write. The greatest improvement is for the person grading the exam. Many students write illegibly and it is extremely time consuming to try to understand what students are trying to analyze or theorize when you simply cannot read their handwriting.

Technology has made the practice of legal research much faster and easier in some ways; we are able to send e-mails, conduct electronic discovery, and find cases quickly online. Researchers and lawyers use blogs to share research information with people who are located all over the world; indeed, the interdisciplinary aspects of the research process have greatly improved thanks to the Internet. However, there is also a lot more information to sort out, and you often get a lot of false hits; therefore, it is important to fully analyze the data that you find, and make sure that you are using reliable sources. This is accomplished by turning to the databases whose business relies upon making sure that their information is correct, LexisNexis, Westlaw, and Loislaw, and official state Web sites and home pages that state they are the official Web site for that entity.

Faculty, students, and attorneys are probably better served using the print materials to perform research in statutes and regulations. It is also easier to use print materials when you are unfamiliar with a topic or unsure of the area of law or subjects that surround the area you are researching. Law review and law journal articles are very easily searched in online databases as well as other types of secondary sources; newspapers and interdisciplinary journals are very easy to keyword search electronically. Cases are also easy to search online using keywords and are very quickly accessed if you know exactly which case you are looking for. Your best researchers, however, know how to use both and quickly find that there are gaps in their research when you only use one type. To fill in those gaps, and to make sure you haven't missed that important case or statute, it is essential to be proficient at performing research using print and electronic sources.

Developing Curriculum for Key Practice Areas

Librarians or directors often serve on law school curriculum committees and assist the faculty in implementing certificate programs, and courses within the curriculum that guide students into specialized areas. For example, a librarian may have expertise in elder law and may teach the research portion of an elder law course. Many librarians who have both an MLS and J.D. degrees are involved in curriculum development and can often contribute their ideas and own experiences as practicing attorneys to the discussions of the committee.

As international law or environmental law programs and courses are expanding, librarians with some subject matter interest or expertise are essential. A faculty services research librarian, instructional services librarian, and information technology librarian are ideal people to focus in growing areas. They can be involved in assisting faculty in the creation of a Web site or collection development in the specialized area. All of these activities are integrated into the curriculum and provide students with an enriching experience in key practice areas.

Another aspect of curriculum reform involves integrating legal research instruction into doctrinal courses or clinics. Librarians are often called upon to give lectures in classes on the various resources that are available in the library or on the Internet that coincide with the material discussed in the course.

Law practice technology is a key area that needs to be added to law school curriculum. Whether this is taught by librarians or technology staff is debatable. Librarians would be ideal because many have the skill set and some have the practical experience. A great deal of law practice technology is based on information management. It mirrors the basics of the information transfer cycle of creation, organization, dissemination, and destruction of information. Case management integrates documents, calendars, contacts, and procedural requirements, which are the nuts and bolts of legal practice. An attorney who uses a case management system is at less risk of legal malpractice. Items, people, and activities are less likely to fall through the cracks if attorneys utilize a good case management system.

Librarians are uniquely positioned to understand and explain concepts like case management, document file formats, and electronic signatures to law students. Electronic discovery, paperless office systems, and security are also areas that librarians may be quite effective in training future lawyers.

In the courtroom setting, knowledge of presentation software has its own set of best practices. It is imperative that we integrate courtroom technology courses into the law school curriculum. These courses must teach future lawyers to present evidence, exhibits, documents, pictures or diagrams using cutting edge technology. Being the tech-savvy lawyer could make a difference in winning or losing a case. The paperless office addresses expensive storage of client information, boxes and boxes of closed cases or client files, and makes the information in the documents more accessible. Although some documents will have to be kept in paper in format, digitizing some of the documents will save money on storage and space, which is at a premium. Having a paperless office makes it possible to have a mobile office. The trend toward mobile offices, while allowing attorneys to work on the fly from anywhere, requires close attention to security issues so that client information is never compromised.

Students who are exposed to law practice technology courses will be able to incorporate technology into a highly effective practice that meets ABA ethical standards. Librarians, IT staff, and faculty can collaborate to provide a complete understanding of law practice technology and its role in modern legal practice.

Helping Students Transition from Law School to Law Firm

The law school library plays an important role in helping the school's students make the transition from law school to law firm. For example, a head of public services librarian could create a packet of information for third year law students that is aimed at keeping them connected to the library—its resources and Web site—after graduation. In addition, librarians could conduct special classes on how to do research online or use print materials in a law firm setting. If you are lucky enough to hire a librarian who has previously worked as a librarian in a law firm and has worked with new associates, it is an excellent idea to utilize their experience. They have special insights and expertise in terms of knowing what skills law students will need to have going into a firm, and can offer that expertise on a one-on-one basis.

As part of this type of librarian's real-world analysis approach to research instruction, they can explain that even though law students are accustomed to having free access to certain databases while in law school, that will not be the case when they work for a law firm. Students moving from law school into a firm or agency learn that they have to break out of the pattern of using only Westlaw and Lexis when they conduct research, and if they do have to use those resources, they are taught that there are ways to get in and out of those databases very quickly. Learning these research strategies can be very beneficial for both the students and the law firms they join, whether they are small, medium, or large, and they are equally useful if they decide to hang out a shingle and practice on their own.

Most importantly, it is essential to emphasize to students that they can always call on their library's services after they graduate if they have questions or run into trouble in the research process, or they can come into the library and can receive assistance finding solutions to their problems. It is important to create a strong relationship with students while they are still in law school so that they know that they can call or e-mail the reference staff once they are out in the real world and that we will still be responsive. Establishing goodwill between the law school library and the student body often goes a long way; indeed, we never know when our graduates might be able to do us a favor as well in the form of making a very large donation to the law library. Building a donor base is always in the mind of directors and law librarians.

In order to help our graduates maintain a connection to the library after graduation it is a good idea to provide a free one-year membership to your "Friends of the Law Library" or fundraising organization for the library. The students get a preview look at books in the book sale prior to the official sale. They receive free document delivery service the first year after they graduate. They also receive free bar review material and assistance with any type of material or forms they may need to transition into real live practice. This is yet another service that helps students to identify librarians as people who can support and help them when they are out in the marketplace.

Benchmarking Your Performance as an Educator

I believe that all librarians are concerned about evaluation; I always look very closely at my student evaluations, and I listen to what students have to say about my class and my teaching methods. Student evaluations are still the major benchmark of a law librarian's performance as educator; it is important to know how students view your course and what they get out of your class.

I also seek feedback through one-on-one conversations with students and colleagues, and I read outside literature to see what other people consider benchmarks in this area. The most important standard of measurement or evaluation of an entire library is a survey or feedback instrument. These instruments can be placed at a circulation or reference desk. Patrons and students are asked to "tell us how we are doing." Usually these surveys consist of anywhere from five to twenty questions about library service and the user's needs, and gives them an opportunity to give suggestions about the physical space, collection ideas, and any type of information they think we should have.

Financial Responsibilities of Law School Librarians

The issue of managing a law library budget is almost solely the responsibility of the law library director, as opposed to other librarians. It is extremely difficult and challenging to meet all of the needs of your constituency, including your students and faculty, with a limited budget. Most of the students who use the law school library have no idea how much books or databases cost, and I do not think that the budget should be an issue for them. When students come to the reference desk in their first year to tell us their needs, the furthest thing from their minds is the cost of materials and the price of databases. It is nonetheless our role as educators to make sure that the library can provide all of the resources that they need.

Therefore, we have to make good, cost-effective choices about what library resources will best meet our students' needs—and it is actually the faculty who are more apt to complain if we do not have the resources they want; faculty members often make it clear that they want certain resources, no matter how much they cost. Conversely, most students come into the library with their own computers, and once they get their Westlaw/Lexis password, we do not get a lot of demands or complaints. Many students who come from a huge undergraduate library setting are also very pleased with the smaller, more personal setting that exists in a law school library. With the rising cost of print and online databases, it is essential that we cease duplication of all sources, turn to free online governmental information, and provide access to the information. We no longer have to own the material, we merely need to provide access to it.

Important Areas of Expertise for Law School Librarians

International and global issues in general are moving to the forefront of legal education, and there are many other specialized areas that law librarians must increasingly be aware of. Fortunately, we are able to obtain a great deal of expertise and understanding of various areas of the law through our primary library contact service; a librarian who works with tax professors in their research efforts on a regular basis will naturally develop some expertise in that area.

I always encourage librarians to go into areas that they are interested in, based upon their experiences and backgrounds, whether it is business, international, tax, or criminal law. It is not unusual for librarians to take courses or continue their education. Librarians who are business-oriented often go on to earn MBAs. Government documents librarians often gain a natural expertise in legislative histories or tax because so much of that information is actually housed in government documents. Other librarians have come into the profession with real-world experience in numerous fields. Law librarians often have several degrees, including Master's degrees in various areas, public administration or literature, biology, the possibilities are endless; therefore, they can assist faculty members with research in those specific or interdisciplinary areas. It is always beneficial to match up a librarian with a faculty member who has a shared subject matter educational background or interest. It is also a good idea to sometimes match up new librarians with new faculty because there is a special bond for people who are new to the institution. They can learn, and work together to learn the landscape of the university and the law school together.

Looking to the Future

The future of the law school library lies in the area of information management—how to manage information, not how to buy books. We need to know how to find the most reliable information sources; and we are moving primarily in the direction of providing access to information as opposed to purchasing it, or leasing it, and housing it. Simply put, we are working to find reliable legal information sources and then finding the best ways to package them for the consumer.

However, information management can be a challenging issue when you are dealing with so many different constituencies in terms of age and skill sets. A law library deals with people from age twenty-one to 101, and everybody has a right to access information in the way that is easiest for them. Therefore, the librarian has to know whether to recommend databases, books, or other types of research materials, based on our various library user's needs and skills.

In many ways, law libraries are becoming information centers as opposed to big research spaces. Indeed, many law firms have gotten rid of their libraries; rather, they are hiring librarians who are able to handle information management. Law has become such an interdisciplinary practice that information management is just as important as librarianship or library science, and librarians are increasingly tasked with specializing in certain areas, and then rearranging and repackaging information to meet the needs of their patrons and constituents.

It can be very challenging to balance the needs of all of your users. A student may come in with a research question, and even if there is a book that can help them, they just want to use a database. However, the next person who comes in with a research problem may not want to go online; they may want a book or something else in hand. Knowing how to manage the many categories of information and the different formats that it comes in is crucial; and meeting the needs of many different types of learners and learning styles is very challenging.

As our population and society becomes more diverse, as new ideas and global thoughts permeate our marketplace of ideas, our institutions must be free and open, progressive and willing to let libraries set the pace in providing information to all who come in our doors or access us through the Internet. The Internet has made our doors now open twenty-four hours a day and seven days a week.

"We have our feet in two different worlds—the world of print and the world of digital or electronic information. So we must plan for the present as well as an unknown future." (Penny A. Hazelton, *Configuration of the Law Library of the Future, in The Future of Law Libraries*, A collection of articles from the 2005 Symposium from a symposium on the Impact of Technology on Law Libraries and Law Classrooms of the Future. March 10-11, 2005, Amelia Island, Florida.)

Joyce A. McCray Pearson came to the The University of Kansas law library in 1994 as electronic services librarian. In 1995, she was named the associate director of the library and in 1997, she became director of the law library and associate professor of law. She teaches independent research, advanced legal research and law and literature. She has published extensively in both law and librarianship and is active in national and regional law library associations.

Professor Pearson is a member of the American Association of Law Libraries; International Association of Law Libraries; Mid-America Association of Law Libraries; Kansas Bar Association; Indiana Bar; and Judge Hugh Means American Inn of Court.

Professor Pearson received her M.L. from the University of Washington, her J.D. from Washburn, and her B.M.E. from Wichita State University.

Dedication: *I would like to dedicate this chapter to my family, Mitchell, Joel, Magan, and Darion Pearson*

Constant Mission:
Changing Methods

Janis L. Johnston

Director, Associate Professor of Law and
Associate Professor of Library Administration
Albert E. Jenner, Jr. Memorial Law Library, College of
Law, University of Illinois at Urbana-Champaign

ASPATORE

Responding to Present and Future Challenges

Fundamentally, I believe that the law librarian's role is to strengthen and deepen the intellectual life of the law school. Teaching faculty has this responsibility as well, but they are encouraged to do so through their teaching and individual scholarship. The librarian has the task of supporting and encouraging the entire community to engage in intellectual inquiry. We do that by creating libraries that engage with faculty and students at every level; that offer resources and services to uncover new ideas; and which expose our users to new approaches in their thinking.

In the past, we managed this task primarily by building collections of materials in-house, and by providing some level of content access through our catalogs. While we still do that, increasingly our role is one of making connections for our users by enhancing their skills in using the tools we make available. We are definitely moving away from the past role of intermediary in the research process to that of educator in terms of training our users to find and evaluate information on their own.

Teaching Key Skills to Law Students

There are several key skills that a law librarian is responsible for teaching their students:

- How to use critical thinking skills in every step of the research process. You can never be intellectually lazy when doing research: that is the primary message that I send to my students at all times. I spend 25 percent of my time in this area.
- How the legal system is organized, including sources of law and court hierarchy (15 percent).
- Learning to be efficient and effective by taking time to understand their research assignment—how to get started; how to finish; the end product expected; and how to be organized during the process (10 percent).
- Comparing efficiencies and results in using print and online sources; how the display of information affects understanding (5 percent).

- How online tools work—Boolean searching, etc. (10 percent).
- How individual print tools are organized and updated, for example how the U.S.C.A. is organized by subject into fifty titles and updated by replacement volumes, pocket parts, pamphlets and USCCAN(10 percent).
- The cost of legal information in print and online (5 percent).
- Updating, updating, updating! The law changes constantly making it imperative for students to rely on the most current information. (10 percent)
- When are you "done?" (10 percent)

I believe that the hardest thing to teach students is that no part of the research process is mechanical. You must always be thinking about how to frame your queries and how to evaluate the results you get. You cannot let programmers or editors make choices for you without thinking through the problems and issues for yourself. When Shepard's or KeyCite flags something, you cannot simply accept that opinion—you have to look at the cases themselves. Perhaps a case is flagged as overturning a previous decision, but in reality, it only negates a part of the opinion leaving the rest of the case valid. Good research takes thought, thoroughness, and time.

The other concept that is very hard to teach—especially to first year students—is when to quit. Most of their weekly exercises are designed to lead them to "answers," but in real life, there are not always answers. That makes it important for us to teach students how to have enough confidence in their skills to understand when they have done enough. It is also very helpful for them to know how time and resource costs will affect how much effort they can expend. Lawyers don't want to spend more money on research than the client wants to spend. These concepts are new to many students, who are both highly motivated and anxious about doing well.

Best Practices For Teaching Research Skills

Between reading their textbook, participating in weekly exercises, and a few in-class lectures, my students have lots of opportunities to take in information, but learning requires thinking through that information to understand how all of the pieces in the legal research process make up the whole. In order to enhance that process, we have frequent review sessions that I model after game shows. For example, we play "Millionaire Attorney;" "Legal Research Idol;" "Legal Research Survivor;" etc. I draw names out of a basket, ask the student a question, and then depending on their answer and the game, they can ask for a lifeline (another student to help), or their answer gets voted on by the class. They get candy and bargain basement pens, etc., as prizes.

The real value of playing these games is that they prompt the students to think about the questions and the answers—and often the initial question prompts more questions about how a particular resource works. It is an active learning strategy that really works and that the students enjoy.

Monitoring Student Progress

In the past, I have monitored student progress by having students submit weekly exercises that have them work with individual types of research sources, e.g., statutes, codes, secondary sources. That tells me if they are learning the rather mechanical process of working with the tools, but it does not tell me if they are "getting it." Therefore, my colleagues and I who each teach a small group in first year legal research are going to try something new next fall. Our plan is to create our own exercises that guide students through working with each type of research source, and then we will ask some questions that require the students to think through how the new source that they have just learned about works with the sources they have learned about earlier. We will also ask questions that require the students to evaluate such issues as print vs. online research; various case-finding methods; etc. Our goal is to help our students to think more critically about how to perform effective and efficient legal research.

Underachievers are fortunately few in our student body, but when they do appear there are several strategies that I use. The first time that they make a mistake, I simply ask them to redo the assignment. If subsequent assignments reflect poor performance, it is time to meet with the student and talk about why they are having difficulty. If it is an attitude problem, then I simply make them aware of the consequences of not taking the course seriously, but more often, the problem is simply a failure to grasp some aspect of the work. If that is the case, I suggest some further reading/assignments, and work with the student to bring them up to speed.

More commonly, I encounter students who are investing too much time in doing their legal research assignments. I try to talk with those students to help them recognize that perfection is not expected or achievable. At some time or other, we all need some coaching on time management! Young attorneys need to know when they are given an assignment how much time they are expected to devote to a particular research project. From that information, they can plan a research strategy that will get results in what may be a very limited amount of time. But perhaps the most important advice I give my students is to document all the steps in their research. There is nothing worse than to arrive at the end of a complicated research project and not remember if you have Shepardized a case or statutes. You don't want to waste time having to redo steps.

Key Library Resources

I believe that the most important resource in the law school library is the librarian. Formats change, collections expand or retract, but the intellectual ability and training of law librarians will always be the key to a successful library.

When it comes to information resources, it is very hard to define which are most important, because so much depends on what the user wants or needs to know. Certainly, both Westlaw and Lexis offer databases of primary and secondary legal sources that are essential to all law libraries. In terms of print resources held within the physical library, code sets are probably the most important. They are essential to contemporary legal research, and are more easily used and understood in print format. Code chapters are arranged hierarchically and are often lengthy. Individual code provisions can only be understood in the context of the larger chapter. Print sources make it easier to see the hierarchy and to flip from one section of the code to another. Online it is very easy to get to the specific, but not see important related information.

Financial Issues for Librarians in their Role as Educator

The financial issues for librarians today are huge. The price of legal information in print form has far outstripped any academic library's budget growth. In the role of educator, we are being driven to teach online sources only—we are not there yet, but getting close. More and more sets in print are being canceled, which makes teaching basic concepts in print very difficult. While most of our students will work primarily, if not exclusively, with online sources when they are in practice, there are some advantages to introducing new sources and concepts with print tools. Some print tools, such as topic outlines in digests, have a much more informative visual display in print than their online versions. For some sources, the print layout helps students see specific information in context of the larger section. Online is good at taking you right to the specific, but students new to the law need to understand how the specific fits in the larger context, and that is easier to display in print. However, that is a luxury we will not enjoy for much longer.

Whether using print or electronic sources, it is imperative that we teach our students to be cost effective. Their time is money—and their time online is money, too. Acquiring and housing print collections is expensive as well. Therefore, we need to be sure that our students understand the costs of doing research—both in terms of the price of owning or accessing information, and in learning how to effectively manage their own time as well.

The primary costs associated with teaching have to do with how my time is spent. If I am preparing for class, in the classroom, meeting with students, or grading papers, then I am not doing other important tasks like running the law library—and unfortunately, there usually is no one else around that can pick up those tasks for me.

Primary Areas of Expertise for the Law School Librarian

Librarians need to be great teachers. More and more of what we do is not related to finding information for our faculty and students, but rather teaching best practices and methods in researching on their own. The days of the librarian as intermediary are behind us, but we still have a vital role to play in training students to be experts in locating information, and evaluating the information they find.

How do you become a great teacher? Practice, practice, practice! There is no substitute for time spent in the classroom. That is where your students will tell you by their reactions, their questions, and ultimately their test scores, what is working and what is not. However, you can also take the time to observe excellent teachers at work, and take the occasional seminar on improving teaching skills.

Good teaching takes a great deal of time, especially the time that is needed to prepare for each class. The more that goes into preparation—updating your knowledge of the sources, developing questions that will lead students to a deeper understanding, planning active learning exercises—the more your students will learn. A good teacher also needs to stay abreast of advances in technology, like wikis, podcasts, and blogs, etc. Using technology effectively can augment teaching, and offer students multiple options to match their learning styles. For example, some students are visual learners so a PowerPoint presentation with good diagrams might be much more helpful than a verbal description.

Helping Students Transition from School to Law Firm

Ours is a law school that focuses more on honing our students' intellectual rather than practical skills in preparation for practice, although we do offer a number of skills courses likes trial advocacy and clinic work. I think that reality presents the library with an opportunity to fill a gap for students in terms of getting ready for their first professional job. I believe that it is very important for the law school and the library to do what they can to help students succeed.

To that end, we offer an advanced legal research course that has been very well received, to the extent that we will be offering a second section next year. We are also starting a series of informal, small group training sessions on a wide variety of research skills (e.g., Boolean searching; business research; tips on using specific databases).

We also always send the message that the first friend a student should make in a firm is the law librarian—and if there is no librarian, we are still here to offer guidance.

Ensuring Portability of Learned Skills

The goal today is not to teach the mechanics of how to use a particular research tool. Research tools, whether in print or online, are not static, but rather are constantly evolving. Five years ago, everyone was still teaching students how to use Shepard's in print, now my library doesn't even subscribe to print copies of Shepard's anymore. Using Shepard's or Keycite online is a snap compared to the cumbersome print process. Yesterday's research process might be very different by tomorrow.

What is portable is an understanding of the elements of the research process; the need to examine all the primary sources of the law to complete a thorough job; the advantages of using secondary sources to understand the law; the fundamentals of Boolean searching; and the necessity of using the most up-to-date information available.

Doing refresher classes in the spring; adding pathfinders to the library's Web page; online chat; etc., are all techniques for reinforcing learned skills so that they can be translated to the work environment. Knowing how to perform specific searches on one database or another is helpful, but the odds are that the search process will have changed in some way between the time you are first exposed to it in law school, graduate, take the bar, and then actually start working in a law firm. Furthermore, the environments in which our students work (large firms, government, solo practice) are pretty varied, as are the tools their workplace will be able to afford for conducting research.

Looking to the Future: Upcoming Changes in Library Science

One of the big changes on the horizon in the area of library science will involve managing digital materials. Bibliographic control has been so important to our past, but we have not produced any reasonable equivalent for dealing with digital materials. One of our fundamental responsibilities is preserving information for future generations, and we must have some way of organizing what is out there so that we can make good decisions about making digital information permanently available. It is a major challenge!

Much of our ability to preserve and make accessible digital information will depend on technology, but more importantly, it will depend on the recognition by all producers of information that some mechanism for systematically preserving digital information needs to happen. We have to figure out how to develop consistent processes and standards; how to do so affordably; and decide who will be responsible for this task so that we can be sure it gets done.

Unfortunately, I believe that we will find that there will be a period—from roughly 1995 to whenever we finally get this digital preservation process figured out—during which a great deal of important information will have simply vanished into the ether. Librarians will need to advocate for digital preservation; learn how to do it themselves; and engage in establishing the systems and standards required.

Janis L. Johnston is director, associate professor of law, and associate professor of library administration at Albert E. Jenner, Jr. Memorial Law Library, College of Law, University of Illinois at Urbana-Champaign. Professor Johnston received her M.S. in library science from the University of Illinois and her J.D. cum laude from Indiana University, Bloomington. She was director of the Marion County Law Library in Indianapolis, and rural development coordinator for the Indian Institute of Cultural Affairs, Bombay, India, before joining the library faculty at Indiana University.

Prior to coming to Illinois in 1999, she was the associate director of the Kresge Library at Notre Dame Law School and taught courses on legal research and the American legal system. In addition, she served as director of the Notre Dame London Law Center for two semesters, with additional responsibilities as interim assistant dean, acting associate dean, and acting director of the law library.

Professor Johnston is active in regional and national professional associations and is a past president and former treasurer of the American Association of Law Libraries. She has authored several articles and regularly gives presentations on law library management and legal information policy. Her article, "Managing the Boss," won the Law Library Journal Article of the Year Award in 1998

Teaching Effective Legal Research

Darla Jackson

Head of Reference and Access Services

Oklahoma City University Law Library

ASPATORE

At the "Teaching the Teachers: Effective Instruction in Legal Research Conference" held at Tarlton Law Library in October 2007, Sir David Williams, Emeritus Vice Chancellor, University of Cambridge, told a story about a radio conversation of a U.S. Naval ship with Canadian authorities off the coast of Newfoundland that went something like this:

> Americans: Please divert your course fifteen degrees to the North to avoid a collision.
> Canadians: Recommend you divert YOUR course fifteen degrees to the south to avoid a collision.
> Americans: This is the Captain of a U.S. Navy ship. I say again, divert YOUR course.
> Canadians: No. I say again you divert YOUR course.
> Americans: THIS IS A U.S. AIRCRAFT CARRIER. WE ARE A WARSHIP OF THE U.S. NAVY. DIVERT YOUR COURSE. MEASURES WILL BE UNDERTAKEN TO ENSURE THE SAFETY OF THIS SHIP.
> Canadians: This is a lighthouse. Your call.

Sir David William's point was that context is important.

Context - An Overview of the Instructional Opportunities for Law School Librarians

I concur with Sir David William. Context is important; and I begin by trying to provide contextual information about the opportunities for law school librarians to serve as educators.

The instructional opportunities for librarians in academic institutions vary significantly from institution to institution. At my current institution, the advanced legal research courses are the sole responsibility of the law librarians. Our staff team teaches two advanced legal research courses each year. Because we are responsible for the design of the courses, the provision of instruction, and the assessment, it is in these courses that our role as educators is perhaps most fully developed.

Law librarians also provide a significant amount of instruction as part of the first year legal research and writing program. Legal Research and Writing (LR & W) instructors who are considered faculty members, but who are not in tenure positions,[1] are primarily responsible for the LR & W courses. Most of the LR & W faculty have significant legal practice and legal writing experience; however, they have not had advanced education in legal research beyond their law school research courses. By invitation from the LR &W faculty, the law librarians provide a significant portion of the legal research instruction on topics such as reporters and digests, statutes, citators, secondary sources, administrative law, and legislative history. The law librarians do not, however, participate in the preparation or selection of texts containing research exercises. Nor do the research librarians review student-completed research exercises, or memo or brief assignments.

While some institutions also encourage the law librarians to teach substantive legal courses, this opportunity is not available at other schools. However, the law librarians may be invited by faculty to provide subject specific research instruction in upper level courses. For example, the tax and administrative law faculty members may dedicate one class session to research and request that librarians provide research instruction during that class session.

The role of the law librarians as educator may not be limited to the law school. Law librarians may be asked to teach in other university schools and departments. For example, law librarians may serve as instructors for schools of library and information science. In fact, the Conference of Law Library Educators (COLLE) was established as a caucus of AALL "to provide a forum for librarians and others who teach law librarianship and legal research courses in graduate schools of library and information

---

[1] LR & W faculty are often given lesser status than the faculty who teach substantive courses. Legal research instructors are often relegated to an even lesser status and are classified as staff rather than faculty. As Roy Mersky notes, "Legal writing instructors have often been treated like poor relatives of the law school. But as bad as that position and status may have been within the law school community, the teaching of legal research, eclipsed by legal writing, was for some time relegated to an even lesser position." Roy Mersky, *Legal Research versus Legal Writing Within the Law School Curriculum*, 99 LAW LIBR. J. 395, 396 (2007). For a thorough discussion of the status of the Legal Writing staff see Susan Liemer and Hollee Temple, *Did Your Legal Writing Professor Go to Harvard?: The Credentials of Legal Writing Faculty at Hiring Time* BRANDEIS L. J. , forthcoming, available at:
http://papers.ssrn.com/sol3/papers.cfm?abstract_id=1033477&download=yes

science"[2] Teaching in the library and information schools may also lead to opportunities to recruit new law librarians into the profession.[3]

Some law librarians may teach undergraduate courses for schools of library and information science.[4] I find that teaching undergraduates assists me in understanding the research skills of entering first year law students. It also forces me to keep up with the current development in information literacy instruction and technology.

So far, this overview has been focused on formal instructional opportunities. However, as Warren Rosmarin, for whom a teaching excellence award has been named, once noted, the classroom is but one opportunity for teaching—there are many others. "Small groups in the Library, or one person at the Reference Desk or at the soda vending machine, all afford 'teaching opportunities.'"[5] Our reference workload always increases when the first year law students have research exercises due. I view these questions not only as invitations to provide additional legal research instruction, but also as an opportunity to seek feedback on the instruction that the librarians have provided in the classroom.

This overview, with minor exceptions, has also primarily focused on opportunities for providing legal research instruction. Ruth Levor, associate director of the University of San Diego School of Law Legal Research Center, in The Unique Role of Academic Law Libraries, points out that the "dimensions of our teaching roles" go far beyond legal research. Academic law librarians' teaching roles are increasing as they are involved in interdisciplinary research, and assisting law students in developing critical thinking and linguistic skills.[6]

---

[2] Conference of Law Library Educators, About the Conference, available at http://lib.law.washington.edu/colle/ (last visited April 14, 2003).
[3] James Milles, *Law Librarians as Educators and Role Models: The University of Buffalo's JD/MLS Program in Law Librarianship*, AALL SPECTRUM, July 2004, 20.
[4] I serve as an adjunct instructor for Acquiring Knowledge in the Digital Age, an online information literacy course offered by the University of Oklahoma School of Library and Information Studies.
[5] Warren Rosmarin, *Teaching Legal Research, The First Column: The First Class*, 11, no. 1/2 LEGAL REFERENCE SERVICES Q. LEGAL REFERNCE SERVEICES Q. 167 (1991).
[6] Ruth Levor, The Unique Role of Academic Libraries: Toolkit for Academic Law Libraries Academic Libraries Special Interest Section American Association of Law Libraries, available at http://www.aallnet.org/sis/allsis/toolkit/unique_role.pdf (last accessed April 13, 2007).

In addition to interdisciplinary research, law librarians are also increasingly encouraged not only to support the empirical research of law faculty but also to engage in their own empirical research.[7] Additionally, they may be called on to provide instruction and compile biographies regarding empirical research.[8]

While this overview reflects the current opportunities available, the overview is by no means meant to communicate that the educator role of

---

[7] "There is a tremendous need for good empirical research on how legal information is used by novice and expert researchers, and on how to teach skills of legal information management and use. Much of the work that has been done so far consists of borrowing scholarship on adult learning and 'applying' it to law students, lawyers, and law faculty, without much inquiry into specific disciplinary communities or practice involved. Library directors should do what they can to promote research in these areas, either by doing it themselves or by supporting their librarians in pursuing such work." Posting of Jim Milles to http://outofthejungle.blogspot.com/2005/08/law-prof-hiring-trends-and-law.html Aug. 2, 2005, 6:12 PM EST). Susan N. Lerdal, *Evidence-Based Librarianship Opportunity for Law Librarians?*, 98 LAW LIBR. J. 33 (2006) also encourages law librarians to undertake empirical research. While some law libraries, are hiring Ph.D. candidates in other disciplines to assist in empirical research instruction, other libraries are involving law librarians. See Duke Law School Library, Empirical Research Support, at http://www.law.duke.edu/lib/facultyservices/empirical (last visited April 13, 2007) and Milles, *supra* note 3, at 22, describing a new course that will offer students "the opportunity to work closely with one of the law librarians as a research assistant on an empirical research project conducted by the librarian."

[8] In February 2008, Law Librarians discussed the increasing demand for empirical research assistance in an online forum sponsored by the AALL Academic Law Libraries Special Interest Section Faculty Services Committee. Although entitled "Supporting the Interdisciplinary and Empirical Research Needs of Law Faculty," law librarians also shared information regarding the increasing instructional opportunities created by the growing student and faculty interest in empirical research. A transcript of the discussion is available at:
http://www.aallnet.org/sis/allsis/committees/faculty/discussion/interdisciplinary-empirical-research.pdf. One example of law librarian contribution to empirical research includes the University of California Los Angeles School of Law *ELS Bibliography Database,* http://www.law.ucla.edu/home/apps/els/ The project was supported by the "hard Work" of law librarians from both UCLA and Cornell University. University of California Los Angeles School of Law, *ELS Bibliography Database Description* http://www.law.ucla.edu/home/index.asp?page=2691 (last visited April 3, 2008) Examples of law librarian instructional products include the Illinois Institute of Technology Chicago-Kent College of Law Downtown Campus Library, Empirical Research Tutorial http://library.kentlaw.edu/tutorials/EmpTutorial/index.htm (last visited April 3, 2008) and the Georgetown University Law Center, *Empirical Legal Studies Research Guide,* available at:
http://www.ll.georgetown.edu/guides/EmpiricalLegalStudies.cfm (last visited April 3, 2008).

librarians has not and will not continue to change. As evidenced by a brief review of Dennis Sears's article, "The Teaching of First-Year Legal Research Revisited: A Review and Synthesis of Methodologies," law librarians' role as legal research educators has significantly changed since the late 1970s when librarians were "limited to overseeing the updating" of the book that served as a self-guided research manual.[9] In addition, as legal research becomes more complex,[10] additional opportunities for law librarians to serve as educators will likely continue to grow.[11] Further, if legal research becomes a subject on the bar,[12] the likely added emphasis on legal research will also likely result in an increase in instruction opportunities. Law librarians must define what we will do with these increased opportunities to overcome the currently existing challenges to effective legal information literacy instruction.

Defining Legal Information Literacy Instruction (LILI)

Legal information literacy instruction is simply instruction designed to help legal researchers develop skills so that they can identify, locate, evaluate, and use information efficiently and effectively. Legal information literacy instructors are concerned not only with teaching students how to select the appropriate sources for researching a legal topic, but with helping the students develop an understanding of basic principles of searching for

---

[9] Dennis S. Sears, *The Teaching of First-Year Legal Research Revisited: A Review and Synthesis of Methodologies*, 19 LEGAL REFERENCE SERVICES Q. 1 (2001).

[10] "Arguably, legal research skills are becoming even more important to lawyers as the legal information environment become more complex and costly. More choices must be made among resources and methods. More discernment is necessary in evaluating information that is available from a wide variety of sources ..." Steven Barkan, *Should Legal Research be Included on the Bar Exam? An Exploration of the Question*, 99 LAW LIBR. J 403, Spring 2007. Similarly see Milles, *supra* note 3, "... with the legal information environment becoming ever more complex, many predict that the need for law librarians will grow."

[11] However, it is interesting to note that Bob Berring, in Thomson West, Research Skills for Lawyers and Law Students (2007), available at http://west.thomson.com/pdf/librarian/Legal_Research_white_paper.pdf, at 8 notes that Harvard Law, as part of its first year curriculum reform, has reduced its legal research training. This change was made despite acknowledgements, from Harvard Law graduates, that legal research skills had not been acquired in law school. (The Research Skills for Lawyers and Law Students is a white paper circulated in conjunction with the AALL Town Hall Forum at the 2007 AALL Annual Meeting.)

[12] See Mersky, *supra* note 1, at 395 and Barkan, *supra* note 3, for discussion of plans to include legal research on the bar.

information, and the importance of strategies for discovering how to use new resources when the researcher encounters these new resources in the future.[13]

Challenges to Providing Legal Research Instruction in the Law School

This section addresses some of the challenges for legal information literacy instructors. When possible, recommendations regarding how to overcome these challenges have been provided.

Time

The challenges to providing effective legal research instruction in the law school environment are many. One challenge is finding the time to prepare and deliver effective instruction. Like their counterparts at firms, academic law librarians must continually work to balance their various responsibilities. Fulfilling reference responsibilities, professional development and writing requirements, collection development responsibilities (particularly in light of the explosion of both print and electronic sources), and administrative duties (including resolving personnel issues and budgeting for both print and electronic resources in a time when budgets seem to be shrinking and costs are increasing) can easily fill an academic librarian's day.[14] In addition to these responsibilities, academic law librarians are increasingly being tasked with copyright compliance issues.[15] Time becomes an issue when the additional responsibility of providing legal

---

[13] These are the concerns of all information literacy instructors, regardless of their specific discipline. Esther Grassian and Joan Kaplowitz, Information Literacy Instruction: Theory and Practice, 9. For a discussion of Legal Information Literacy, see also Richard Danner, Contemporary and Future Directions in American Legal Research: Responding to the Threat of the Available, 31 INT'L. J. LEGAL INFO. 179 (2003).

[14] Mary Whisner, *What do you do all day?* 94 LAW LIBR. J. 661(2002).

[15] As the AALL Academic Law Libraries SIS Faculty Services Listserv Discussion" Law Faculty, Copyright and Law Libraries", May 2-3 2007, Summary, available at http://www.aallnet.org/sis/allsis/committees/faculty/discussion/copyright-discussion.pdf, illustrates, academic law librarians are responsible for a wide variety of duties involving copyright, from Interlibrary Loan and web course postings to requesting copyright permission for course packs.

research instruction is added.[16] Notwithstanding, academic law librarians have recognized that they must undertake legal research instruction.[17]

Assessment

Another challenge is to find the time not only to prepare and deliver the instruction, but also to assess the effectiveness of the instruction.[18] Assessment is perhaps the component of information literacy instruction (including legal information literacy instruction) most often overlooked. Writers on information literacy instruction point out that "many factors contribute" to the failure to undertake "rigorous assessment … in the IL field."[19] These factors include a lack confidence that assessment can be properly accomplished; an unwillingness to expend time or money on assessment development; and a reluctance to reduce the amount of material that can be included in order to provide sufficient time for assessment.[20]

By necessity, the continuous debate regarding the best pedagogical approach for legal research instruction has also included discussion on the best method for assessing the selected approach.[21] Confidence that

---

[16] Academic librarians have continually battled with fitting all of their tasks into the available time. Often librarians who teach, provide reference, and are engaged in publication to fulfill tenure responsibilities, must devote significant personal time to research, writing, and preparation for instruction. Danielle Hoggan, *Faculty Status for Librarians in Higher Education.* 3 LIBRARIES AND THE ACADEMY 431, 438 (2003).

[17] For example, see Herbert Cihak, *Teaching Legal Research: A Proactive Approach*, 19 LEGAL REFERENCE QUARTERLY 27, 35 "I stand with those who believe that librarians who fail to respond to the metamorphosis in the information environment face extinction. Taking a proactive approach to teaching legal research is one step down the road to survival." However, Michael Lynch points out that academic law librarians, because of their experience with scholarly research, which "emphasizes the comprehensive search for all relevant sources over the struggle to understand authorities that are found in the context of a restricted problem controlled by client's interest … may be too hopeful regarding what can be achieved in law school." Michael Lynch, An Impossible Task but Everybody Has to Do It - Teaching Legal Research in Law Schools 89 LAW LIBR. J. 415, at 421.

[18] Lynch, *supra* note 17, at 433. Lynch notes that an increase in research assignments would required a substantial investment of instructor time for not only preparing the exercises but providing feedback.

[19] Esther Grassian and Joan Kaplowitz, INFORMATION LITERACY INSTRUCTION: THEORY AND PRACTICE, 269.

[20] Id.

[21] See for example, Paul Calister, *Beyond Training: Law Librarianship's Quest for the Pedagogy of Legal Research Education*, 95 LAW LIBR. J. 7 and

assessment of legal research instruction and student legal research skills can be properly accomplished has been, as discussed below, adversely affected by the integration of legal research and writing instruction. Recently, legal organizations outside academia have also begun to express doubt about whether an effective assessment tool for legal research skill can be developed.[22] *Best Practices in Legal Education*[23] suggests that if it is not "feasible" to accomplish some assessment, law schools should not stop trying to achieve "desirable outcomes" but should "be realistic about what we can assess and whether it is imperative that we do so."[24] While assessment of legal research instruction may be difficult, it is imperative that we continue to work to create an instructional environment that will encourage valid assessment rather than adversely affect it.

Assessment, in situations in which legal research and writing are integrated and responsibility for legal research instruction is shared, is particularly difficult. Yet this model is quite pervasive in law schools. The Association of Legal Writing Directors/Legal Writing Institute Survey for 2007 reported that only fifty-four schools teach legal research separately; while 149 law schools integrate legal research and writing. Further, in 2007, sixty-one schools reported that they utilized a combination of librarians and LR & W faculty to provide legal research and writing instruction. The number of schools reporting this approach has increased significantly since 2004, when only forty-nine schools reported using a combination of legal writing instructors and law librarians to provide LR &W instruction.[25]

---

[22] In 2006, the President of the National Conference of Bar Examiners (NCBE), Erica Moeser, in announcing that the NCBE was in the "first stage" of considering the idea of testing legal research skills as part of the bar, acknowledged the difficulty of "devis[ing] a test delivery mechanism that serves our purpose [to assess if the examinees have the legal research skills required of an entry-level lawyer]."Erica Moeser, *President's Page*, B. EXAMINER, May 2006, at 4, 5.

[23] Roy T. Stuckey et. al, BEST PRACTICES FOR LEGAL EDUCATION: A PROJECT OF THE CLINICAL LEGAL EDUCATION ASSOCIATION (2007). Available at http://cleaweb.org/documents/Best_Practices_For_Legal_Education_7_x_10_pg_10_pt.pdf (last visited April 13, 2008).

[24] Id. at 253.

[25] 2007 survey results reported in Majorie Crawford, *Bridging the Gap Between Legal Education and Practice: Changing the Way Legal Research is Taught to a New Generation of Students.* April 2008 AALL SPECTRUM 10, 11. The complete survey results, including comparative information regarding results in previous years is available at http://www.alwd.org/surveys/survey_results/2007_Survey_Results.pdf

When law librarians teach most components of legal research but are not responsible for reviewing student performance on legal research exercises, memos, or briefs, it is difficult to assess the effectiveness of the training and to modify future training to more adequately meet student information needs.[26] Further, given the traditionally different approaches to legal research instruction taken by law librarians and legal research and writing faculty, if responsibility for assessment is placed on the shoulders of the often already overburdened L R & W faculty, it is likely that the selected assessment tool may not correspond or will not meet the goals of the material covered in the instruction.[27]

In-class exercises may provide a means of addressing the varied learning styles of students as well as a means of obtaining feedback from students when, because of the combined L R & W faculty and law librarian teaching situation, the librarian has limited additional access to the students. However, even this means of assessment may impose some difficulties. For instance, if law librarians are given only a limited amount of time (fifty minutes in many cases) to discuss statutory research, after presentation of the material, which must include print as well as electronic access to federal and state statutes, there may be very little time in which to engage the students in meaningful exercises. Further, as noted by Michael Lynch, the

---

[26] For example, Patrick Meyer, Associate Library Director at Thomas Jefferson School of Law, notes that it was the grading of assignments that lead him to conclude that "it can be a tricky proposition to conduct proper legislative code research online." Thomson West, Research Skills for Lawyers and Law Students (2007), at 6. Available at http://west.thomson.com/pdf/librarian/Legal_Research_white_paper.pdf (The Research Skills for Lawyers and Law Students is a white paper circulated in conjunction with the AALL Town Hall Forum at the 2007 AALL Annual Meeting.) See Grassian and Kaplowitz, *supra* note 19, at 285, regarding whether "product assessment" is an effective means of judging the quality of information literacy skills and instruction. Product assessment "can be a useful way to determine what students have accomplished; but it does not indicate how they got there. We make the assumption that a good product means the process was followed." Further, using product ssessment does not sufficiently clarify "whether it was our instructional intervention that contributed to the end product or some other influence."

[27] See Lynch, *supra* note 17, at 431, "I offer only two observations. If librarians are the ones teaching legal research, more information about the sources will be presented, if no absorbed, in the course. If legal research and writing instructors control the syllabus, however, the time devoted to legal research sources will inevitably decline."

knowledge demonstrated by exercises is of a nature that it will not be "long retained without reinforcement."[28]

Additionally, we must consider that even when there is not shared responsibility for instruction, librarians may have difficulty fitting assessment into the instruction plan. Law librarians do not often share responsibility for advanced legal research courses in foreign, comparative, and international law (FCIL) research. Yet, as discussed at the 2007 FCIL Special Interest Section's Teaching Foreign and International Research Interest Group, because students are not familiar with the political and legal systems of foreign jurisdictions, some instruction regarding the systems and tools to use to develop contextual understanding is a prerequisite to additional research instruction. However, discussion of this necessary information fills a significant portion of the limited class time that might otherwise be used to complete exercises that reinforce the instruction.[29]

Information literacy advocates, such as Ester Grassian and Joan Kaplowitz, authors of *Information Literacy Instruction: Theory and Practice*, propose what seems like a simple solution to the problem of "too much" content and limited retention. The simple solution is to select a limited number of "transferable concepts and illustrate them using the resources you have selected to present."[30] Grassian and Kaplowitz acknowledge that there may

---

[28] While speaking about library exercises rather than in-class exercises, Lynch, *supra* note 17, at 435, notes that exercises can be "simple and quick to correct." However, he also notes that the knowledge demonstrated by such exercises is often not retained.

[29] While the uninitiated might expect that similar legal and political system instruction would not be necessary when teaching U.S. law students U.S. legal research, I anticipate that their expectations would require modification. To many law librarians the *Schoolhouse Rock – I'm Just a Bill* video is an essential tool so that law students who have never had a civics class can understand the lawmaking process in the U.S.

[30] Grassian and Kaplowitz, supra note 19, at 9. "Overkill is under learning; the more you pour in, the less that will be retained. After all, you do not want your users to think that being information literate is unattainable." Despite cautions not to make information literacy appear to be unattainable, law librarians do appear to have unrealistic expectations about the depth of understanding that law students can attain. Lynch, supra note 17, at 421, observes that librarians "may be too hopeful regarding what can be achieved in law schools." Similarly, if legal information literacy professionals cannot set forth the core competencies for legal research in less than 108 pages, students may certainly believe that legal information literacy is unattainable. See CORE LEGAL RESEARCH COMPETENCIES: A COMPENDIUM OF SKILLS AND VALUES AS DEFINED IN THE ABA'S MACCRATE REPORT (1997), prepared by the American Association of Law Libraries' Research Instruction Caucus.

be a "time and place" for instruction about the "mechanics of a particular system." However, they suggest that mechanics may often be addressed through print or electronic supplementary materials.[31] Further, because, particularly in the case of electronic databases, the interfaces seem to change with regularity, instruction about mechanics becomes rapidly outdated. Reducing the amount of content may result in improved retention of important concepts and allow time for the additional formative assessment, which includes feedback that is "provided primarily to support students' learning and self-understanding rather than to rank and sort."[32] Increased formative assessment is recommended in *Educating Lawyers*, one volume in a series of reports on professional education prepared by the Carnegie Foundation for the Advancement of Teaching. Student questions at the reference desk may, in some situations, also serve as a means of assessing how effective the formal legal research instruction has been. In addition to serving as a means of assessment, answering reference questions may provide opportunities to provide some reinforcement of the information with which students were familiarized during the formal classroom instruction.

Student Styles and Skills

Although this is not unique to legal research instruction, it is a challenge to develop instruction that appeals to and takes into account the learning and thinking styles of our diverse students. Unlike professors in other disciplines, both the substantive law faculty and legal research instructor are not required to take educational courses as part of their graduate programs. Additionally, most will not have served as graduate assistants and may lack classroom experience. Without a background in educational concepts, legal research instructors may find that developing instruction addressing student learning styles is difficult. For example, without a familiarity with learning styles, a legal research instructor might not appreciate that both in-class exercises and library exercises might be necessary to motivate impulsive learners, who "find quick accomplishment rewarding;" and reflective learners, who must work slowly and "consider alternate solutions."[33]

---

[31] Id.

[32] William M. Aullivan et, al. EDUCATING LAWYERS: PREPARATION FOR THE PROFESSION OF LAW (2007).

[33] Grassian and Kaplowitz, *supra* note 19, at 62.

Further, the instructor might not appreciate that individuals selecting a specialization in the social sciences tend to have diverging learning styles and are inductive reasoners. As a result, rather than systematically constructing a search strategy, they would prefer to begin keyword searching and figure out a search strategy based on the results of the search.[34] Because beginning a keyword search without a strategy would likely be inconsistent with the approach suggested by the legal research instructor, if there is to be any hope of modifying the behavior, legal research instructors must provide additional explanation of the approach they are suggesting.

Developing an appreciation of student learning styles is often an outgrowth of developing knowledge of the students themselves. While law librarians may engage in activities, including participating in the first year orientation program, serving as liaison or judge for moot competitions, and answering questions at the reference desk, without significant modification of the current instructional environment, it will be difficult for the law librarian to develop a knowledge of students similar to the knowledge that the L R & W and other faculty have. This is due in large part to the fact that the law librarians do not have daily teaching interactions with the students and, as previously discussed, do not have access to or provide feedback on student assignments. Without the opportunity to engage more thoroughly with the students, the law librarian cannot foster the type of mentor-mentee relationship, which best practices for legal education suggests fosters student growth.[35]

Finally, teaching effective legal research requires that law librarians overcome the common misconception that everything is available electronically and can be easily accessed by someone with adequate computer skills. Because most law students have grown up using computers and Internet search engines, they have the experience of retrieving a variety of information sources with little effort. As a result, they mistakenly believe that they are effective and efficient researchers.[36] Their experiences with computer-assisted legal research (CALR) often reinforce this.

---

[34] Id. at 63, 74.

[35] Stucky, *supra* note 23, at 118.

[36] Mersky, *supra* note 1, at 399; Shawn Nevers, Candy. *Points and Highlighters: Why Librarians, Not Vendors, Should Teach CALR to First Year Students*, 99 LAW LIBR. J. 757, 768 (2007).

Recently, I had a conversation with a first year student who was suggesting that we offer CALR training to older alumni. I happened to be in the computer lab scanning a document when she was having difficulty manipulating text in a file. I offered my assistance. My success at helping her with this simple task apparently established my credibility as a skilled technology user. Thus, she began a conversation stating that anyone who had graduated more than "five or so years ago" likely did not have CALR instruction in law school. (Obviously, her timeline for the introduction of CALR into the law school was inaccurate.) She had met with a group of older alumni and she was concerned that they were "spending way too much time doing research in the books." I shared with her my agreement that instruction in electronic legal research would be a good idea for our alumni. Further, I had actually offered a CLE course on electronic research, although not including Westlaw and Lexis. She was pleased. I then seized the opportunity to offer, however, that not all research sources were available electronically, and that some attorneys, particularly those familiar with a specific area of practice, found book research more efficient and less costly. I brought home the point using the example of specific secondary sources. She seemed amazed, and indicated that this was certainly a new idea for her. Although the law librarians had repeatedly explained this in the first year research sessions, her experience may have prevented her from hearing us.

This anecdote makes the point of how important it is for librarians to have the opportunity to interact with students and to introduce them to the idea of using an integrated approach to research that considers print and electronic sources. However, even this may not be enough. Returning to the idea of context with which this article began, Barbara Bintliff, in her article *Context and Legal Research*, suggests that the law has undergone "a series of revolutions," and so must legal sources.[37] Bintliff asserts that these "new textbooks" of the law "must be designed for research in an electronic environment" and must "organize and structure the fields of law."[38] Today's law librarians are experts in the structure of information and we are leaders in the area of technology. Perhaps one of our new educational roles may be to work with both the academic law faculty and the practicing bar to

---

[37] Barbara Bintliff, Context and Legal Research, 99 LAW LIBR. J. 249, 265.
[38] Id.

devise these "new textbooks" that will meet the expectations and needs of our students.

Conclusion

While opportunities to fulfill the multi-dimensional teaching roles appear to be expanding, academic law librarians must nonetheless enlist the support of legal writing faculty, law school administrators, and others to ensure that legal, interdisciplinary, and empirical research instruction does not receive less attention than it deserves.[39] Effective teaching and reinforcement of research knowledge throughout the three-year law school experience requires a significant commitment of time. All of the constituencies in the law school community must be willing to support such a commitment. Such a commitment is unlikely without the voice of the practicing bar, as consumers of the law school product, demanding improved research skills from those entering the legal profession.

Academic law librarians must not forget that instruction opportunities are not restricted to the classroom. We must be prepared to provide such instruction at the reference desk or wherever and whenever it is requested. Additionally, we must call upon our own practice experience as well as developing relationships with law firms (and the law librarians they employ) and legal information vendors to ensure that we are providing research instruction that is relevant to the practice environment that our graduates will encounter.

Further, we must not lose sight that we must establish relationships with our students. These relationships will not only improve the law school experience for our students but will provide opportunities for us to assess the effectiveness of instruction. Further, these relationships will serve to create additional educational opportunities

---

[39]Faculty have previously viewed traditional legal research more as a practical skill that is not of sufficient educational value to justify the expenditure of all too precious resources. The inclusion of empirical research, often viewed as more scholarly, but also as having practical value as an area of research instruction, may also facilitate more enthusiastic support from the regular law faculty.

Finally, we must seek out opportunities to expand our roles as educators. Involvement in creating the "new textbooks" of the law seems to offer such an opportunity that is well suited to our skills and knowledge. Leaders in the law librarian community are encouraging us to share a vision of the future in which we have successfully participated in "revolutionizing the law school curriculum so that law scholarship and law practice have the benefits of the information explosion that will no doubt continue unabated well into the century."[40] Working with diverse groups within the legal community, we have the ability to make this vision a reality.

Darla Jackson is the head of reference and access services at Oklahoma City University Law Library. She team teaches two advanced legal research and writing courses, and serves as a guest lecturer in the First Year Legal Research and Writing Course. She also serves as an adjunct instructor for the online course Acquiring Knowledge in the Digital Age offered by the University of Oklahoma School of Library and Information Studies.

Ms. Jackson earned a Juris Doctorate and Master of library and information studies from the University of Oklahoma. She holds a Master of Law (international law) from the University of Georgia. She has also earned a Master in military operational art and science. Ms. Jackson is admitted to practice in the state of Oklahoma. Prior to embarking on a career in law librarianship, she practiced law in the United States Air Force and taught at the U.S. Air Force Academy Department of Law.

Acknowledgment: *Thanks to Karen Kalnins for proofreading the early draft of the chapter. Thanks also go to Lee Peoples and Judith Morgan for providing encouragement and time to write the chapter and for sharing their ideas on teaching legal research.*

---

[40] Mersky, supra note 1, at 401. We must recognize that a revolution of the current "conception" of legal education will have to be undertaken. JAMES R. MAXEINER, EDUCATING LAWYERS NOW AND THEN: AN ESSAY COMPARING THE 2007 AND 1914 CARNEGIE FOUNDATION REPORTS ON LEGAL EDUCATION, viii (2007) succinctly summaries the situation. "[w]hile legal educators may hope that the latest Carnegie Report on legal education will bring about a similar blossoming of legal research and clinical education, their hopes are likely to be dashed. Alas, the PPP Report is not likely to change the face of legal education. Contemporary conceptions are too constrained for that. Although enhancing social science research and clinical education in law schools has broadened the understanding of the role of American law schools, that broadening has been accompanied by a narrowing of the horizon of legal education generally."

Teaching the Questions, Not the Answers

Christopher Simoni
Library Director and Professor of Law
Drexel University Earle Mack School of Law

ASPATORE

Introduction

Law librarians have always been involved in the educational and research missions of their law schools, whether through building collections, providing one-on-one instruction, teaching courses in legal research, or writing legal research treatises. The great ones often did all four simultaneously.

In recent years, law librarians have become even more directly involved in their law school's educational mission. There are several possible explanations for this—as the legal information environment has become more complex, it has become vital for law librarians to master and then to share their deep knowledge of these resources with students who will find themselves, just a few short years after entering law school, with no understanding of the complexities of legal research, in practice needing to know how to use those resources effectively.

The practice of law has changed, too, placing a greater emphasis on the bottom line, reducing the quantity and quality of mentoring available to new associates. One consequence of the change is that newly minted attorneys are expected, more so than in the past, to be able to produce, and produce effectively, from the time they walk in the door. This pressure to produce has created opportunities for academic law librarians who can step into this gap and, with their colleagues in the legal writing programs, help prepare students to be effective and efficient researchers in the law firm environment.

The legal publishing industry also has been in a state of flux, first with the transition of materials from print to a print-electronic hybrid information environment, and then with consolidations in the industry, with well-known resources changing as they are acquired by a different publisher, or in some instances disappearing entirely. This latter problem has been compounded with Westlaw and LexisNexis, the two major online legal services, where materials that are on one or both of the services one day, may disappear the next, because of changes in licensing agreements.

Finally, the range of information attorneys need to know, from the hard sciences, to economics, to psychology, simply expands the universe of information that attorneys need to know how to find, analyze, and use. We are in an information rich environment and those who are adept at effectively and efficiently finding, filtering, and analyzing mountains of data will have a competitive advantage over those who cannot do so with the same skill and ease, and law librarians have a central role to play in helping students become adept researchers in this environment.

The Road Taken

My career in law librarianship began not in libraries, but in law school teaching. Upon graduation from law school, I taught in and directed a legal research and writing program at Willamette University College of Law in Salem, Oregon, where I also taught, at different times, torts, environmental law, and administrative law. Although the substantive classes presented teaching challenges, none were as difficult to teach well as legal research.

In 1987, I had the opportunity to go to Austin, Texas, and work for Prof. Roy M. Mersky, an acknowledged leader among academic law librarians, and the director of the Tarlton Law Library at the University of Texas School of Law. While at Tarlton I enrolled in the University of Texas School of Information Studies, receiving my M.L.I.S in 1989. During my three years at Tarlton, Prof. Mersky repeatedly reinforced the central role that law librarians had in teaching law students (and faculty) the importance of legal research. In doing so, he gave me a variety of opportunities to merge my experience in law teaching with law librarianship and, with the talented law librarians at Tarlton, the opportunity to develop the first advanced legal research courses taught at the University of Texas School of Law.

After leaving Tarlton (although those who worked for Roy Merksy never really surrender all ties to him and Tarlton), I have held various positions and library directorships at both research and smaller academic law libraries, sometimes teaching, sometimes not. After ten years as director of the Pritzker Legal Research Center of the Northwestern University School of Law, I seized the opportunity in 2006 to become the inaugural law library director at the newly founded Earle Mack School of Law at Drexel University in Philadelphia.

The decision to move to Drexel was not made lightly. Among the factors playing a role in the decision was Drexel's strong history of co-op education, a hallmark of the university that would play a significant role in the law school mission. The School of Law offers students a variety of co-op opportunities in law firms, business, government, the courts, and the nonprofit sector that provide real-world professional experience.

With its strong co-op program and focus on melding legal theory and practice, Drexel offered a significant opportunity to develop a law library from the ground up that would play a significant role in helping to educate students to become effective legal researchers and well-regarded attorneys. All other things being equal, students with strong research skills will be at a competitive advantage in their co-ops.

Teaching the Questions, Not the Answers

There are a variety of ways one can teach legal research and I have tried most of them at one time or another with varying degrees of success. The approach I use today, one that is consistent with my understanding of learning theory, combines elements of legal bibliography, process, and skills in a way that, when it works, enables students to develop and *internalize* a legal research heuristic or set of questions (not answers) they can use as a mental checklist as they approach a research problem. The checklist helps them get started in their research, no matter what the subject, and can help keep their research on track.

Although legal bibliography has gotten a bad name in some circles and can conjure up visions of librarians fascinated with legal arcana, the more arcane the better (and I plead guilty to this particular offense). Legal bibliography, however, is only part of the equation. For it to be meaningful to today's students, I find it helpful to teach it in the context of the process of legal research, that is to say, knowing how to put the pieces together into a coherent whole. The final part—skills—integrates the legal bibliography, the process, into an effective method of research.

Over the years, I changed and modified the checklist and it now has a strong process orientation with questions the students are supposed to ask of their research plan and resources at key decision points. Those questions are key to me, for they require students to understand that effective legal research is not a rote undertaking.

The questions tell the students to identify for each research problem that makes the law, i.e., are they looking for statutory, regulatory, or judicial resources (or a combination of the three); how they make it; where they publish it; what's the publication pattern (e.g., slip law, session law, code); how are the resources updated. For secondary materials the questions focus upon matters of coverage or scope (i.e., does this resource deal with the subject I'm researching); using the resources; and currency (including frequency and means of updating). Finally, the students are taught to ask how the primary and secondary materials work together.

While it is not possible in the average advanced legal research course to point out all (or even many) of the differences between print and electronic resources (and it would be a fool's errand to attempt to do so because the content and character of the resources are in a state of flux and yesterday's description of the contents of a particular digital database is likely to be wrong in some particulars), one can teach the students a series of questions they can use to "interrogate" the products (and formats) under consideration to help them chose the most appropriate tool.

Good legal research instruction also will disabuse students of the naïve belief that digital information resources always are better than print information resources. This is a point librarians can reinforce in teasing out the differences between free resources on the Internet in comparison to fee-based resources such as Westlaw and LexisNexis. We also need to teach the students to "question" the online commercial resources. For example, it is not uncommon, given the complexities of licensing, to find that some law materials in print are more current than their online versions on Westlaw or LexisNexis. This happens frequently enough that students should be alert to the possibility and remember to "interrogate" the resources about their currency. Only by teaching students to use a critical approach such as this do we teach them research skills that they can use in different areas of the law, using different types of materials.

The question of cost-effective research is of paramount importance but is, unfortunately, difficult to teach in the academic setting because we lack the appropriate incentive structure to make students internalize the importance of selecting the proper tool for the task at hand.

One sees the importance of this cost-effective research in law firms from the types of questions attorneys and law firm librarians frequently ask academic law librarians. Five years ago, a typical question from an attorney or a law firm librarian to an academic law librarian was along the lines "Why do students use only Westlaw and LexisNexis research?" Implicit in the question was the concern that students were losing something by not "using the books" and what was lost was efficiency, a lower cost, and perhaps better results.

While one still hears that question today, it has been overtaken by a more nuanced one that asks, "Why are students not more effective in using Westlaw and LexisNexis for research?" To me, the difference between the questions is telling, and signifies an important change in how some attorneys perform research and, accordingly, what they expect from new attorneys. To see that this change is more than a local phenomenon, one need only review the finding reported in the 2007 ABA Legal Technology Resource Center Survey that found a steady increase in the number of attorneys, regardless of years in practice, who are moving to online research with the majority of the respondents expressing a preference for online resources.

The questions that I try to get my students in advanced legal research to internalize require them to have a good understanding of the underlying information resources, because without that they will not know either what questions to ask of the resources, or how to evaluate the "answers" they receive. Consequently, when we teach advanced legal research, we spend a significant amount of energy ensuring that students not only know what types of materials are available and how to use them, but also how to determine currency and completeness when comparing and contrasting them against alternative information resources.

If students can master the publication patterns of various types of legal materials, e.g., statutory materials, they can carry that skill over when they have to research administrative materials. While there is little that is directly transferable from statutory research to administrative research, the similarities in the publication patterns in the primary materials are close enough that students will know what types of questions to ask about what resources are available. Students tell me this does help them in the transition to law firms.

Staying Current

The legal information environment is changing as much for law librarians as it is for students and for academic law librarians to remain effective and relevant teachers they must stay informed about the changes in legal information and the changes in the practices and preferences attorneys. I like to be informed about where our students are clerking, what practice areas they're working in, and what types of research problems they're working with. When possible, I try to speak with the firm librarians about the types of research done at the firm and whether the librarians see any changes in how research is being done. For teachers of legal research, the law firm librarians can be among the best early warning system for changes in how legal research is conducted in the real world and our teaching will benefit to the extent it remains relevant to the skills the students needs to succeed.

What It's All About

Ultimately, the best researcher is an informed researcher who chooses the proper research tool for the problem at hand. In the end, the best law librarians can hope to accomplish when teaching legal research is to introduce the students to the variety of materials that exist, the ways in which types of resources differ from others in material ways, and how to choose the right tools for the task at hand.

This is a good time to be an academic law librarian. So much of the received wisdom about what it means to be a law librarian and educator is being contested (which always makes things interesting). This is also a good time to be an academic law librarian because the skills we possess as a group, make us excellent teachers and those skills now are more in demand than before.

Christopher Simoni, library director and professor of law at Drexel University Earle Mack School of Law, has played a role in modernizing academic law libraries in the United States, and his areas of interest include information policy and copyright and the evolving nature of research communities.

Professor Simoni came to Drexel from Northwestern University School of Law, where he was associate dean for library and information technology and professor of law and director of the Pritzker Legal Research Center. While at Northwestern, he developed a library-faculty liaison program and the Pritzker Faculty Research Fellow program, and led the transformation to a combined print and digital collection. He also coordinated electronic publishing initiatives and was responsible for managing the law school's journals, helping get three new student edited journals launched and on the Web. At Northwestern, he taught advanced legal research and researching the scholarly paper.

Previously, he was an assistant professor of law and library director at Marquette University Law School. At Marquette, he taught legislation and advanced legal research. Before going to Marquette, Professor Simoni served as the associate director for public services and, for a while, acting library director at Northwestern and before that as assistant director of the Tarlton Law Library at the University of Texas at Austin. Before beginning in libraries, he was associate professor of law at Willamette University College of Law, teaching legal research and writing, torts, administrative law, and environmental law.

A member of the Law Library Microform Consortium board of directors, he serves as vice-chair of the Facilities Committee of the Legal Education and Admissions to the Bar Section of the American Bar Association. He previously served on various ABA committees including the Law Libraries' Committee and the Questionnaire Committee, and has served on a variety of committees of the American Association of Law Libraries.

He completed consultancies with law libraries at the Addis Ababa University in Addis Ababa, Ethiopia, and the University of Ghana in Legon, Ghana, advising them on the uses of information technology as one means of increasing access to legal information.

Professor Simoni received his M.L.I.S. from the University of Texas at Austin, his J.D. from Lewis and Clark College, Northwestern School of Law, his Ph.D. and M.A. from Marquette University, and his A.B. from the University of Michigan.

The Law School Librarian: Filling in the Gaps

Darcy Kirk

*Associate Dean for Library and
Technology and Professor of Law*
University of Connecticut School of Law

ASPATORE

The Librarian

The law school librarian's role in law school education has changed dramatically. I have been an academic librarian since 1971. In those early days, librarians were in the back rooms handling books. They were rarely seen or heard. Today, they are very much involved in the law school and collaborating with deans, faculty, and staff to provide a well-rounded education for the law students. For example, here at the University of Connecticut, the new president has just released a new university plan that he is calling an academic plan rather than a strategic plan. Each school and department has been asked to develop its own plan that will stem from or coincide with the university academic plan. As soon as that plan came out, I was e-mailing the dean here at the law school, reminding him that the law school library is an important part of the law school's academic mission and that I was interested in helping him prepare the law school's plan. We continue to be in touch, thinking about the future of the law school, what direction it is heading, and how that direction coincides with the university's plan. So, the librarian is right there, helping to formulate that plan and thinking about the law school's strengths and who and what resources within the library can help support those strengths and the direction the law school takes.

One of the reasons for this change of role for the librarian is the competition for money. When law school deans look at how much they spend on library resources, they cannot overlook the fact that it is a significant percent of the overall law school budget. So, they ask, "What am I getting for that money?" And they further ask the librarian to spell out that value. The library director and staff who are savvy enough to realize that their dean will ask them to justify what they are spending money on are already out there touting their work. So, that changing role is partly being driven by not wanting the library's budget cut. But there are other more significant factors that have moved the librarian from the back office to leadership in the law school's educational mission. Probably one of the most important factors is technology. Since I began as a librarian, technology has taken over in the work of the librarian. Research and legal research, in particular, is technology driven. Indeed, everything that a person touches today involves some form of technology. But it is these changing times with technology that have thrust the librarian and libraries into a critical central role in law schools. Libraries now have a significant leadership role to play through technology. It all started in the library with the online catalogue and then Lexis and Westlaw. The smart librarian embraced the emerging technology (instead of hiding in that back room) and ran with it. So, today, that same librarian is looked to for leadership with technology and how it can be utilized throughout the law school to assist faculty, staff, and students in their everyday work. That comfort with technology has, in many instances, added the overall responsibility for directing technology for the law school to the library director's job. So, it is not surprising that the librarian's role has expanded beyond research support to that of helping students and faculty get their work done efficiently and expeditiously—whether it is helping them with a database or a spreadsheet to make their life easier, that is part of our role.

Another factor that has changed in the role of the law librarian is his/her working group. The librarian works regularly with other faculty, staff, and students. Looking back, when I first began, I envisioned the role of the head of the library as a senior position in the law school, but not having a significant role in running the law school. Initially law library directors did not have a title like an assistant dean or associate dean and were not necessarily part of the law school management team. Now, more and more, the head of the library has an associate dean title. Here, I am part of a small management team within the law school. To the extent that the library director is much more aware of what is going on in the law school and plays a role at that higher level, that changing role elevates the importance and impact of the library's part in the educational mission. I believe that is happening.

The successful library director spends time developing multiple relationships. Once I became a library director, people counseled me that I now had multiple constituencies, not just staff reporting to me—that I needed to develop relationships within the faculty and with the management staff and other departments in the law school such as admissions, alumni, etc. All are important pieces of your relationship group, so the more time I spend working on those relationships, the better off the law school is, and the library as well. And over time those relationships have changed, and they help underscore the fact that the librarians are educators.

Those persons within the law school will now turn to the library staff for their educational roles, especially where legal research is concerned.

This year, not only am I busy within the law school, I am also active professionally as a member of the executive board of the AAAL (American Association of Law Libraries). I have many relationships within that professional association and they are very important to me, personally and in my work. I learn from my professional colleagues and bring that knowledge back to my work here. And because of just how dynamic the world is now within librarianship and within the area of technology, you just cannot sit in your office and wait for people to come to you. You have to seek out those relationships and the information while trying not to reach overload. That said, it is an exciting and ever-changing profession and I enjoy every minute (almost).

Students and Education

The librarian's role in helping students to transition from school to law firm is an important one. Over the years that I have been a law librarian, I have been involved in teaching several workshops for law students that assist with that transition. These so-called "bridge the gap" programs provide a training opportunity for law students with what to expect once they reach the law firm setting, especially with research work. At Georgetown, we had a formal, full-day workshop where we had some of our academic librarians and some local law firm librarians working together to present the material. The first half of the day included the academic librarians talking about the basics of various type of research and the law firm librarians talking about research in the law firm and the expectations for research in the firm, including watching time and costs. The second half of the day was devoted to a hands-on exercise on a real-world research problem. Plenty of time was also devoted to questions about everything from dress in the firms to work hours and achieving partnership. Other "bridge the gap" efforts have been conducted over a brown bag lunch or as part of a bigger law school or career services program about preparing to practice. When I teach my advanced legal research class, I invite a law firm librarian to come in and talk about life in the firm, training, and research expectations. More recently, the IT department, which also reports through me, is working with our law school clinics to modernize their use of technology. The clinics, which often act as mini law firms, are a wonderful training ground for law students. So, teaching the use of new technology that is already in use in law firms is another way that we can assist our law students with the transition to law firms and the practice of law. For example, we just purchased case management software for our law school clinics, and we will be training students and clinic faculty how to use it.

I really see the library staff as providing leadership in training in the technology law students can use at law firms. I know that Boston College Law School offers a law firm technology course and that is something we are moving toward. I think the regular teaching faculty do not have the time or the interest to teach something like that. Research skills, clinical skills, litigation skills, all of those types of practical legal skills were previously downplayed as part of the law school education. However, those skills are now much more important and valued as part of preparing the law students so they can hit the ground running when they arrive in the firm. I see the librarian's role as leaders in teaching those skills, as well as pushing skills teaching in the law school agenda.

Ten years ago, I would have said my primary skills teaching responsibility was teaching legal research, but it is so much more now. Legal research, in and of itself, encapsulates many skills; everything from finding the primary materials that students are looking for, to blue booking skills, but even more, it is time management, working expeditiously. One of the big things I do when I teach first-year legal research is to teach them how to know when to stop. Students get carried away with finding cases—the more the better; but knowing when to stop is important, because in the real world their time will be very limited. So I teach them to create and follow a research process or agenda and to prioritize their work so that they still will come out with the best final product while being cognizant of time constraints.

When teaching legal research skills, we introduce law students to the different sources out there to find different types of materials—some might be free, some might have a cost factor; when it makes more sense to use the database and/or the source that might cost, and when it is just as easy and often faster to pull the book off the shelf. Those kinds of skills will be invaluable in the law firm setting. Faculty and lawyers who do research in specific areas of law own or have easy access to the sources that they use all the time, but we introduce students to the breadth and variety of resources that are available to them for many topical areas of legal research. I teach students that when looking for a certain primary source, there may be ten ways to find that source. So, if the firm they are working at does not have the first source that comes to mind, there are other ways to get at that same research. I show them different avenues—teach them a research process, including what comprises a good research process, how to develop it and follow it and how to do it; what is the short version, what is the long version, so at least they are exposed to a step-by-step research process. As I say to my students, "You can write this down or you can put it in your head," but try to go step by step when you are doing it, rather than just immediately "jumping online" to do your research without any prior thought. Take the time to think about what you are really trying to find and what is the final outcome you are looking to have, and also find out how much time you have to do it. We try to provide our students with a comfort level with legal research, with the library, and how to use it, as well as a familiarity with a law library collection in general. Students are less and less likely to come into the physical library, but we help them recognize what is in it and what could be useful to them.

It is definitely most difficult to teach the use of print materials for research because of the negative mindset that exists with today's students toward the use of books. Certainly, in many cases, it may be time to move beyond print versions of some titles, such as the *Federal Register* or the *Code of Federal Regulations*, because many of those titles are available online for free. However, I still prefer to introduce the print versions first. I find that if I can get my students to look at the print version, once they see it in print, how it is laid out, and how the publisher hopes it will be used, they have a better understanding of how to use it online and an easier time doing so. Another difficult area to explain when teaching legal research is the use of controlled vocabularies and indexes instead of straight keyword searching. Today's students are so accustomed to typing in whatever they want when searching that they are reluctant to think about using specific subjects or other specialized topical headings when searching. Sometimes, there is a way of "backing into" using a keyword search. This is the easiest way to teach this method of searching. Once the student obtains the results, they are usually as pleased by the outcome as they are with the research results using the print resources.

Monitoring students' progress as they learn research is an ongoing part of the teaching process when I teach research. They have weekly written assignments, so it is easy to see which students are doing fine and which ones are struggling as well as what are the problems that they are encountering. I encourage them to come and meet with me (and many do), and within the class there is lots of time for asking questions. Because there is time allotted during class for in class exercises and hands-on activities, there are also opportunities for resolving difficulties as they arise. In addition to the weekly exercises, the students are required to write a "bibliographic essay." This essay is a written version of an entire research process—in anticipation of writing a paper or a brief or a memo (that they might do in a law firm). When writing the essay, they are forced to pull together an entire research process, step by step, and in so doing they learn where they are feeling uncomfortable. I meet with them and they can talk through how they envision their research, what sources they plan to use, the steps they plan to follow, and I can call to their attention points they may be missing. The course is entirely interactive this way between professor and student.

When I teach legal research, I lecture and I allow time for hands-on skills learning. We go into the library to find print materials or we sit in class with everyone using a computer and/or I am projecting on the board, so we are all looking at the same items on the screen. Since legal research is a skills-based course, there must be a practical, hands-on component. So, the weekly assignments allow the students to explore the sources that are introduced each week. Those sources may be found in the library (in print) or online in any number of electronic databases. What is especially rewarding for me is their surprise and pleasure by what they find when using the print materials. Needless to say, this generation does not need any encouragement to use online resources, so the research instructor spends more effort leading the students to print and also convincing them of its value. Invariably, most students are very pleased by what they find when using print materials and they will almost uniformly say it was useful for them to know. Some of these books, once the students get into law practice, will make or break their success. Up until that point as law students, they have just been focusing on cases and statutes and becoming familiar with the terminology. They are going to get out there and someone will say "CFR," and they will say, "What is that?" because they did not come across any administrative materials in their first year. So hands-on is vital, and then beyond that, having them follow through on an entire research process step by step. They pick the topic and look at as many materials as they can. Evaluating those materials by looking at a book or an online database forces them to think more like a librarian. They learn some sources are not as good as others are, and there can be some online sources that are wonderful and others that are not valuable at all, because they have to be able to rely on the material.

Technology plays a huge role in educating law students. Even before the law student arrives at the law school, the law school Web site becomes a hugely important tool for information. Students no longer receive the huge packet of information from the law school once they have been accepted and indicate that they plan to attend that school. Instead, they are referred to an admitted students' Web site where all the information that they need to start school can be found. That site which includes such information as financial aid forms, student employment forms, and housing information now also includes information about the library. The library staff is taking advantage of that Web site to communicate with the entering students before they arrive, giving them tips about using the library and information about the kinds of services they offer. Once the students arrive at the law school, there are many ways that the technology is useful, especially with respect to teaching legal research. This is a generation that loves to look at videos, so not just PowerPoint, but video clips and photos can be used in the classroom to help the students learn and engage them more. By the same token, having interactive resources is useful. We now have online chat available with the reference staff. We provide self-service features in our online catalog—renew your books, place a hold on a book. We are investigating other ways to communicate with students using social networking sites. We try to use the same techniques that our students use in their own lives. We also offer most of our electronic resources for offsite use to students at home. We put the information where they are looking to find it, rather than expecting them to come to us. The same holds true with the teaching techniques. Technology can make the legal research more fun—a panacea for the fact that research instruction can be deadly boring.

Difficulties with the use of technology in teaching are several. When the technology itself fails or is difficult to use, the instructor may be disinclined to try it again. We are all nervous the first time we try using a new form of technology in the classroom. When it works successfully, it can be fabulous. When it breaks or just doesn't work, we are often at a loss for a backup method and it is embarrassing. Sometimes the technology requires more training than the instructor has time for. So, the instructor may choose not to use the technology, or worse, attempt to use it and it doesn't work. Further, just keeping up with all the changes in technology can intimidate the instructor and prevent him or her from improving a course or adding new material. A number of our library staff teaches portions of first-year legal research and advanced legal research. There is always something new to be added each year, so the challenge is making sure everyone is comfortable enough with the new database, software package, or projector to teach it or with it. With the rapid development of new databases and software, the instructor has to know how to use it first, requiring additional time for self-training. However, if the new resource were simply a book, the librarian could just open it. I still use a document camera in my class to show books and book pages, because information and organization within the books are useful for the students to know. If you are showing an online database, there could be a glitch with the database itself or the equipments, or what you saw yesterday online may not be there today for a variety of reasons. Thus, for all its glitz, technology is still a bit unpredictable. But we won't stop using it and it still catches the students' attention.

If the library director is smart, he or she can be very successful in leveraging school resources. As stated earlier, it is all about demonstrating the value of the law library to the law school enterprise. Here, we have an insurance law center, which is fully funded by outside grants. A number of faculty salaries are funded through its revenues and it also funds half of a full-time librarian's salary—that librarian is designated as the insurance law librarian. Our international LLM program also funds a half-time librarian. Thus, both programs, which are funded by outside revenues, acknowledge the importance of having specialist librarians supporting their work. They are willing to pay those salaries and they contribute some funds toward our acquisitions of materials on their related subject areas. Another benefit of this funding is the relationships that have been built between the two librarians and the program faculty. Those faculty are exceedingly pleased with research and support we provide their programs and the two librarians enjoy the more intimate relationships they have developed by being an actual and integral part of those programs' staff. In addition, they both teach research skills to the students in the programs and they teach in upper-level classes about the resources in those areas. There is real collaboration there, where the faculty in those areas value and regularly applaud the importance of the librarians supporting their work. Finally, this past year, we have a new program, an intellectual property and entrepreneurship clinic, which is also providing some funding for acquisitions.

That said, the law librarian should be willing to share resources, as well. As print collections in libraries shrink and use of libraries has tapered or declined off, library space has become available or at least desirable by other law school units. The law library here at the University of Connecticut is a very large building—approximately 100,000 square feet. Since I have been the director, I have given up space to admissions, student finance, and most recently, the police department. I do not look on these "takings" as bad for the library but rather it shows our willingness to be part of the solution for space needs in the law school. In addition, these new departments increase the traffic and "bustle" in the library, which I also view as a good thing.

The Successful Library Manager and the Future

Besides the librarian being an educator, he or she needs to be fundraiser. Availability of resources will continue to be a problem for law schools and law libraries, not to mention the fact that acquisitions budgets will never keep up with the rate of inflation for books and electronic materials. So, it is necessary for the librarian to be comfortable with the idea of raising outside money. It is important to work with the on-campus development group, and I work directly with our development head here at the law school. When money is donated to the law school, sometimes the donor would like to give to the library. Rather than wait for that to happen, I speak with the development head about that possibility in advance. She can often recommend avenues for the donor's money. I want the library to be one choice on her list. In addition, the law library director has to be like a CEO. He or she is actually managing a small corporation; it may be small but it is multi-layered with staff, has a large budget, and requires careful planning, in order to manage and direct it properly—all responsibilities required of a modern day CEO. Beyond that, the law library director is also a faculty member. As such, he/she needs to be active professionally, writing and publishing and keeping abreast of all areas, not just law, but interdisciplinary areas that overlap with the law and what is going on in the world of legal education. It is very important to have that broader world view as the faculty and the deans (to a lesser extent) may have a narrower view. So, the library director needs to be more broadly focused to help the law school remain on the "cutting edge" of technology—teaching methods, topical issues or anything else that might have an affect on legal education in general.

Copyright has become more and more important, especially with the online environment. Here we have a whole copyright team at the university level. One of the law librarians participates on it. They have created a whole copyright Web site. We have been working closely with one faculty here to provide support for their publishing and teaching with respect to copyright. This support has included recommendations for what is allowable for course Web sites, retaining copyright in an online publication, etc. We have even given some talks to the faculty about what we believe is reasonable for them to put online, versus when they will need to obtain copyright permission. We also discuss with faculty about learning to hold on to their copyright when and if they can, when they are publishing or putting articles online, especially with all the online services now. So librarians have become the copyright experts on campus and that is an important and good thing. My belief is that whenever librarians can be the "go-to" persons in an area, it makes them valuable and raises their visibility.

Management is an area where many librarians need to develop more expertise, especially if they want to move up the ladder. Even if they do not, I think it is useful to be able to think about how you manage even a small section. For example, if a librarian were head of the reference unit, he or she should prepare an annual plan setting forth goals and steps to reach the goals. That way staff and monetary resources could be efficiently allocated. Staff could be trained for new initiatives and the manager would have successfully moved the section forward while learning effective management skills in resource allocation, planning, and training. Other areas for further development could be subject areas. Many academic law librarians do have law degrees, but it is not a requirement. A master's in another subject area (beyond library science) would be useful if they have an interest. Librarians are generalists—needing to know or be aware of a little about many areas—in order to know what the library user is asking about. To the extent that a librarian can have an expertise beyond just the library degree, it is really useful.

The staff is the most important resource within the library. If you have a good staff, everything else falls into place. Obviously, the collection is important, but if we did not have the staff to access it, catalogue it, or teach about it, then it would be for naught. I am lucky to have an excellent staff, and when I see the faculty on campus or at meetings, they routinely praise the library staff's work. This strong support of the library on the part of the faculty also protects the library from a budget cut. The dean would be hard pressed to cut the library budget when it would run counter to the strong support of the faculty who believe that their success with research and publishing is directly related to the library staff and the library collection, which supports its work.

Monetary resources are obtained through a formal budgeting process within the university. It starts at the law school level and then goes to the main university. Resources are allocated according to university goals as outlined in the academic plan (mentioned previously). There is also a university librarian, and even though I do not report to him, it is important for me to have a working relationship with him. So, if there are budget issues that relate to the university libraries in general, I work with him on those. We generally get an increase to all the library budgets every year, but whenever there is a question about it, or that increase is threatened, we get together to develop a strategy for opposing any elimination of that increase. Politically within the law school, having developed those relationships, I can then support my budget requests. If I want to ask for an increase or a new position, I lay the foundation for the reasons that I might need that additional money, and then I have the law school dean's support to move forward to the provost. By the same token, the opposite happens as well. There is a top-down thing when there is going to be a budget cut. When that happens, I work more closely with the associate dean of finance. We look at ways to cut the law school budget as a whole, where the library may not be hit quite so hard. In our case, we constantly struggle to keep within our acquisitions budget because legal materials are increasing at a faster rate than our budget. So, when there is a question of a budget cut across the university, the associate dean for finance and I work together to figure out ways where we could take that budget cut from lines other than the book budget. Again, having developed a really strong working relationship with that associate dean, I am able to protect what I have.

The aspect of librarianship that will change the most in the future, indeed, is changing now, is the issue of print versus electronic materials in the library collection. It is an area that many librarians are struggling with. There obviously needs to be a balance between print and electronic resources, but what is the right balance? That balance is going to continually change. The balance will depend on dollar resources, staff resources, and space resources. Law firm libraries have opted for getting rid of large quantities of print resources because of the square footage costs. However, many university law libraries are and will remain more conservative and retain the role of what was traditionally called the research library. That research library will still maintain many print materials. Obviously, the balance is going to change, but it is going to be an ongoing discussion, and librarians will need to look at that tension between eliminating the book and not. Technology keeps pushing the role of online in all avenues of the law school. For example, some law schools are going totally paperless with their admissions. Potential students can apply online, but then the admissions staff ends up printing out the file for the admissions committee to read. The concerns here are similar to reading books online. How many people are truly willing to do all their reading online? Thus, how far does anyone want to go toward some sort of paperless library? I do not think we are there yet, so library science will continue to struggle with that balance.

Library schools will continue to need solid training for librarians and use of technology. But, as I mentioned earlier, management skills training also needs to be emphasized. I have an M.B.A. and it has come in handy repeatedly as a manager and now library director. To the extent that librarians can be trained in topics such as budgeting, use of spreadsheets, and planning, it will serve them well in their role as a librarian.

Law students do not want to think about whether a librarian is an educator or not. We should be seen as part of the overall educational process. The library should provide what is needed for the student when he or she needs it. We are on the admitted students' Web site where we make it clear that we are there to help them in whatever way they might need. If we do that right then and gain their trust, they will come to see us once they arrive on campus. Over time, they will view the librarian as someone who helps them really think, articulate a problem and find the solution; someone who helps them with time management. In some ways, the librarian is almost like a social worker. We are there to listen to what is up with the students, to help them balance law school and their lives, to help them to do their research, and help them prepare for practice. So, we are, in some ways, really the renaissance educators. We fill in the cracks from the traditional teacher and traditional professor. We come around the edges and say, "What are you not learning in the classroom?" and ask how we can help them in those areas. As I mentioned previously regarding the case management technology and clinics, how to find a book in the online catalogue, or what to wear to an interview, we can be all things to all students. The smart law librarian steps into the breach in order to be an active participant in the law school's mission and purpose.

Darcy Kirk is presently the associate dean for library and technology and professor of law at the University of Connecticut School of Law. A graduate of Vassar College, she received her law degree from Boston College. Dean Kirk also earned both her M.L.S. and M.B.A. from Simmons College. Before moving to the University of Connecticut in 1996, Dean Kirk worked at Harvard University's Widener Library, she served in several positions at the Boston College Law Library and served as the associate law librarian for public services at Georgetown University Law Center. Dean Kirk is active in many professional organizations including the American Association of Law Libraries (AALL) where she serves as secretary, the New England Law Library Consortium (NELLCO) where she serves as treasurer, and the Law Librarians of New England where she previously served as president. She is a frequent presenter at professional meetings speaking most often on topics related to teaching legal research skills. She teaches advanced legal research and higher education law.

Acknowledgment: *I would like to thank Simon Canick for his advice and suggestions.*

Training the Next Generation of Lawyers: Teaching Essential Research Skills

Patrick Meyer

Associate Library Director and Adjunct Professor of Law
Thomas Jefferson School of Law

ASPATORE

Key Challenges

The academic reference law librarian teaches in one form or another, provides reference services to students and faculty, researches for faculty, and may provide interlibrary loan services to all patrons. The mastery of varied reference skills will enhance the librarian's classroom expertise.

One of the most critical challenges that we face is adequately preparing our students to be an immediate asset in the law firm setting: Academic librarians have first crack at instilling the basics of research into the neophyte student researcher.

Most librarians would likely agree that new attorneys and law students are relying on the Internet for their legal research needs more than ever before. Therefore, it is more difficult to persuade students that books are still relevant. One basic fact is that not everything is online. This author has recently reported that few secondary source loose-leaf treatises are available online. (Patrick Meyer, Think Before You Type: Observations of an Online Researcher, 13 *Persp.: Teaching Legal Res. and Writing* 19 (2004)). (See the discussion on the law firm requirements pertaining to other print resources in the Teaching Primary Research Skills section below.) Even if a source exists in both print and electronic formats, the latter is nearly uniformly *the* chosen access method. Students are able to quickly search through databases and settle on a presumed answer without effort, knowledge of the area of law they're researching, or an understanding of how the resource or database is structured. This is seen as exacerbating the problem of a lack of basic research acumen, as reported by law firms.

The author conducted extensive research over the first several months of 2007 in order to ascertain the research needs of law firms (results are on file with the author; see also the Appendices for some of the research results and comments). Relevant comments from respondents included: "With online research in general a major concern . . . it would be nice if attorneys would not stop . . . their research when they get *any* answer as opposed to the best answer. Too many attorneys don't know what they could be missing, appear to be unaware of the shortcomings of online research and don't have familiarity with the organization of the print materials if they only use them online"; "Anything we can do to teach attorneys (1) not to scorn books (2) not to assume what they find on the free Internet is current and accurate (3) typing a generic subject into [the] allcases [database] on Wexis does not provide the best results . . . ."; "[W]e have to teach new attorneys about the valuable material found in secondary treatises. We have to explain what a TOC [table of contents] is and where to find it. Explain the use of an index. Repeat over and over that not everything is on the computer."; "At our law firm, we think print resources are best when an [attorney] is starting a new, unfamiliar project, or needs to see the "big picture." Online [research] is best when the [attorney] has a good idea of what he or she is looking for. New attorneys seem too unfamiliar with print resources." For more law firm comments, see Appendix A.

One example of how difficult and tricky online searching can be is with the typical legislative code research problem. As we are aware, an act is comprised of several code sections that must be read in conjunction with each other. For instance, you cannot apply the penalty section to your research facts without reading the section that gives the exceptions to the law. These relationships are often hidden from the neophyte researcher in the online environment: A search may retrieve the penalty section of an act but not other critically relevant sections. There is often never a thought to look at how the section being scrutinized relates to the other sections in the act. It is often easier to understand the relationship between code sections of an act—or even to be aware that a relationship exists—using print resources. Identifying the relationship between sections within the same act is easier when using the print legislative code sets, where the table of contents is readily seen. At a glance, you can easily tell that there is, for instance, a section for definitions, penalties, and exceptions. Granted, the ability to view the table of contents of the various code databases does exist in the online environment, but it is often overlooked as it involves an added step to the often preferred online research process.

Users of print resources are guided through the research process by experts in the particular subject that the student is reading about. They know the legal terminology associated with the area of law as well as the law itself, but the neophyte user often knows neither. One starts the process intending to look up certain presumed keywords in an index and finds a better term along the way— either by referral from a smartly cross-referenced index or by serendipity, where they happen upon a more appropriate word while looking up their intended keywords. The worst that could happen is that the intended keyword was not in the index and there was no cross-reference to another keyword. In that instance, the user simply chooses another keyword to look up. Compare that scenario to the more typical occurrence of a student or entry level associate, who is often unfamiliar with the area of law they have been asked to research, typing what amounts to guess words into a search box in an online database. Further, it is difficult for researchers to recognize the necessity of using synonyms, which would greatly enhance the average search. So the use of print resources tends to broaden the researcher's understanding of an area of law well beyond the point of conducting what can easily be the myopic search of the untrained online researcher.

A process that can be extremely difficult for the neophyte researcher to grasp online is that of conducting systematic case law research through digest searching. My experience is that the process is much better understood when taught in the print format and when students are required to complete print digest exercises. With the proper groundwork, digest research online becomes more consistent.

Law firms are reporting with alarm that the new researcher has the dangerous tendency to start a research project in an unfamiliar area of law in the primary law databases. This relates to an issue discussed above in that researchers do not take the time to consult a good practice guide in order to learn the layout and the language of a particular area of law before jumping into their primary law research. This is a typical comment from one of the respondents to my law firm research project: Attorneys "[h]ave no understanding of the need/use of practice material, practitioner based research and resources . . . they always start in case law [databases] on Lexis or Westlaw, [and] don't know how to do much else." The result is that the researcher may mistakenly think that the holdings of the cases that they find relate to the issues they are asked to research.

The traditional method of passive classroom lecturing is not an effective means of teaching today's student. Just as it is for us when we seek training, students must be engaged or they will tune out. Today's students have much more technology at their disposal to divert their attention than many of us had. Such technology includes instant messaging, e-mail or text messaging, the Web (to include MySpace and Second Life) and so on.

Obviously, when you lose their attention, your course objectives are not being met. My philosophy is to spend no more time lecturing than is absolutely necessary, and to provide as much hands-on training as possible during class time. And although the type of class that I teach may not lend itself to the full Socratic Method that typifies law school classes, it may be employed in a modified form. To that end, it is another tool that I may use to keep the class engaged.

On a related issue, most academic reference librarians do not teach in the formal classroom setting, and as a result, it is often a luxury for a law school to be able to provide their students with more than one advanced legal research course a year (which is often taught by the library director). These courses are time consuming to prepare for and to grade, and assignment exercises must be updated each time one teaches. On the other hand, preparing a course and then teaching it is possibly the most effective means for new librarians to quickly develop their reference skills. It is also a major benefit to have on the resume. It is definitely an expectation that needs to be discussed when interviewing to fill a reference librarian position.

There are many opportunities to fulfill the librarian's role of educator beyond the legal writing and advanced legal research courses. Students will have the necessity to research for their paper courses. Students will also work in law firms or for judges during their law school careers. Libraries could benefit by finding ways to be a larger part of this demand for additional research training. A challenge that many academic law libraries have experienced over at least the past decade (and which I am happy to report is not the problem in my school) is how to replace a decline in walk-up reference requests. But such a decline alone does not necessarily signal a failure for the reference department. A helpful way to put this issue into perspective is to view it from the eyes of your patrons. This generation of students has grown up with the Internet and is comfortable seeking answers online, away from the physical reference area of the library. Years ago the user had to conduct research in the library, but often (and with increasing frequency) they are now able to so do online. So the worth of a reference department should no longer be measured to such a high degree by the number of in-person encounters. Still, there are ways to increase foot traffic within the reference department. One such way is to have library staff teach a legal research course. When the student body realizes that a librarian, or the library staff, teach legal research courses, they will then better understand how the librarians can help them in their schooling, as research is a component of the mandatory first year legal writing course. Student will then have more confidence in the skills of the librarians and they will not be as reluctant to approach the staff for research help throughout their schooling. Another means of generating student contact is by offering library tours individualized to the resources used by each legal writing professor. This involves only a small amount of coordination with the professors. Through this contact with the librarians, many students will be more willing to approach a reference librarian afterward, when they are conducting research. They will have gained an understanding of the various types of useful information a librarian can provide to them.

You may want to try to increase foot traffic by offering boot camp and mini-class offerings. Our library has just successfully conducted our first law firm legal research boot camp. The boot camp covered the essential research tasks students need to know as they prepare for their summer clerkships. Subjects covered were federal and California primary law (yes, we included administrative law and court rules!), court filings, citator services (online only), and practice forms. Boot camp consisted of two two-hour sessions on successive days. Each resource was explained, which was followed with short hands-on research exercises. (See Appendix B for sample exercises.) One session was devoted to using the books and the other to using online resources. There are opportunities to develop other boot camps or similar training sessions as well. For instance, we may conduct another boot camp shortly after the bar exam as a means for those who had been occupied with studying for the bar to prepare for the profession as they await their bar examination results. We have also started to offer formal training for law review citation checkers.

We provide roughly thirty legal research mini-classes over the course of each semester (many are repeats). The content of each mini-class ranges from an introductory level to advanced. Classes may be as simple as how to conduct case law or statutory research or how to use one of the practice guide multibases. The idea is to limit each session to one discreet type of research, which keeps the sessions short, and encourages attendance. They are often only fifteen to thirty minutes in length. We strive to make the training process as convenient and accessible to our students as can be. We also try to time the mini-classes to coincide with the time at which students are conducting research in their classes—a just-in-time approach. (The subjects of the mini-classes are of most relevance to the legal writing classes.) Most mini-classes have been digitized and placed on the student Intranet site, in an attempt to broaden the scope of our mini-class offerings beyond the walls of the library. We are in the process of enhancing some of our training videos by showing the accompanying PowerPoint slides alongside the video of the trainer. Along the same lines, we contact the legal writing faculty in an attempt to forge a mini-class training partnership. The most beneficial relationship would be to have the librarian provide just-in-time specific research training either in the legal writing class or in the library stacks. For instance, if the students are about to be set loose to search for case law with their assignment literally in hand, we would show up to provide the appropriate training.

With virtual reference not being a good solution for many libraries who lack the staff to answer reference questions in the time frame expected by our patrons, some libraries are relying on pathfinders that they upload to their library homepage. The pathfinders provide a means of identifying valuable subject-specific research resources are tailored to the particular library's holdings and/or database subscriptions. Our library has produced and digitized dozens of subject-specific pathfinders. This is another example of how to provide reference services beyond the physical confines of the library and at the time when the student is ready to benefit from the information.

Teaching Primary Research Skills

The primary skills that librarians teach to law students are as follows. Note that there is much overlap in the teaching of the various components listed below: They are taught to some degree in each class. Therefore, it is difficult to assign individual percentages:

- The overall research process (35 percent)
- How to conduct specific types of research, such as federal/multi-state/California secondary source, case law, digest, legislative, court rules, administrative law, and legislative history research (50 percent)
- Cost-effective legal research (15 percent)

I have found that the most difficult research skills to teach law students include any that require multiple steps—especially (but not exclusively) tasks to be performed in the print format. Many librarians believe that such difficulty is directly related to an increased comfort with using the Internet in general, and specifically with the use of Google, Westlaw, or LexisNexis, which are seen as one-stop resources. Students are of the mindset that they may find all of the answers online. They seem to be hypnotized by the physical ease of online searching—never thinking about what documents were not retrieved and assuming that the answer they have is the best that there is, or at least acceptable, when it may not be. Impatience also serves to inhibit students from being effective legal researchers. I see students time and again abandon a set of research results without proper analysis because they did not find what they were looking for in the first one or two result summaries. I cannot help but wonder if the immediate gratification they have become accustomed to with, for instance, their non-legal Google search results, plays a major role in this deficiency. This mindset definitely explains the lack of understanding of the research process, which in turn negatively affects the ability to recognize inferior research results, as students are less equipped to discern a good answer from a bad one. In all fairness, however, many students also initially struggle greatly with the several steps required to conduct a successful online search. A successful online search requires the ability to find the appropriate database, choose the correct keywords, synonyms and connectors for the search query, the ability to effectively review the retrieved documents list, a knowledge of how to adequately navigate through the full text of retrieved documents, the ability to synthesize several documents to a research fact pattern, and the ability to update their research. A seemingly insignificant mistake at any one of these steps will result in inaccurate or irrelevant results. In a law firm setting, that is unacceptable.

The specific research tasks that are most difficult to teach include using digests; updating Code of Federal Regulations (CFR) sections; and Shepardizing in print to determine if the case or code section is still good law since it was decided or passed into law. (I do not teach print-based Shepardizing in a formal classroom setting based on my research results; See Appendix C for what tasks law firms feel should be conducted online). It is also difficult to teach the typical research process/progression from using broad secondary sources, to specific practice materials, to primary law; accessing unfamiliar types of databases; and terms and connectors searching, where the user defines the relationship between keywords that must occur in a document in order for it to be included in their search results.

My recent research on law firm legal research needs elicited 162 valid law firm responses. (For a succinct summary of the results, see ThomsonWest, White Paper. *Research Skills for Lawyers and Law Students*, 5-7 (2007)). One purpose of the research was to determine what print format materials were still required in the law firm setting. When asked "[w]hat research tasks should usually be conducted in books vs. online?" over 85 percent chose "secondary source research." Legislative code research and legislative history research also scored high (see Appendix D). These responses strongly suggest that print-based components for secondary source and legislative code research should be taught in legal research or advanced legal research courses—of course, at the same time you're teaching the electronic equivalent.

I asked a complimentary question to the one directly above: "What print resources must entry level attorneys know how to use?" A large percentage of research tasks were chosen by a high percentage of respondents. (See Appendix E.) Here were the top answers:

- State legislative codes (67.8 percent)
- US Code (65.1 percent)
- Federal reporters (53.9 percent)
- Federal secondary source materials (52.6 percent)
- State secondary source materials (51.3 percent)
- State reporters (49.3 percent)
- Federal administrative codes & state digests (47.4 percent)
- State administrative codes (46.1 percent)
- Federal digests (44.7 percent)

Based on my research findings, I am sure to include several print research components in my advanced legal research course.

Another area of training that I am sure to stress is that of cost-effective research. Law firms are reporting that only about 3.5 percent of their so-called "flat rate" contracts are actually unlimited in scope—or truly flat rate. That means it nearly always matters how you perform your online research. (See Appendix F for the breakdown of law firm pricing plans.) In addition, the number and types of functions that you use on this year's plan will be taken into consideration when it is time to negotiate next year's contract.

Although there are variations to the three types of pricing plans, one can teach the general makeup of each plan. I am also careful to point out how to conduct certain functions in the most cost-effective manner. For instance, when you have a citation to a document and would like to retrieve it, you can save quite a lot of money using the "Find" or "Get a Document" command in Westlaw and LexisNexis as opposed to conducting a full database search using the appropriate segment or field. You can also save by navigating the table of contents as opposed to conducting a full database search. Tables of contents are now provided for many databases. You may expand the table of contents until you access the full text of a section, and you are charged at the less costly "Get a Document" or "Find" level once you do so. And of course, there is the old standby of starting with a broad initial search so as to be more certain to retrieve relevant documents, and then using Focus in LexisNexis or Locate in Westlaw to narrow that original group of documents to a manageable number—the Focus or Locate search being free. In that way you decrease your chances of conducting a full database search that retrieves no (or no relevant) documents. Another example of a potentially extreme cost-saving measure would be to use your hourly plan instead of a transactional plan to conduct several simultaneous Shepardizing or KeyCite functions while using WestCheck or BriefCheck.

Finally, I have secured approximate undiscounted database range charges for mid-sized law firms and I include this approximate range in my in-class exercise reviews. See Appendix G for law firm comments as to the reasons for new hires incurring excessive research costs.

Best Practices and Benchmarking for Teaching Research Skills

I use several strategies to reinforce my teaching of basic research skills. First, I rely heavily on hands-on in-class exercises. Each exercise is a series of short questions designed to teach students how to use particular book titles or databases that relate to each lecture topic. I circle the computer lab or accompany students to the stacks and provide feedback when students run into trouble. My students complete at least one in-class exercise in nearly every class. I also provide PowerPoint screen capture exercise reviews to further reinforce the point of the exercises. The reviews give the students a chance to see the process that I used to answer each question— from what databases or print titles I used, to how I accessed the resources, to what terms I used, to how I analyzed my retrieved documents. Students have stated on several occasions that these reviews are of high value. Students not only benefit from timely feedback when the reviews are shown during class, but students rely on them to prepare for the final examination, since I post the reviews to the course Web site. I constantly review my in-class assignment and lecture materials to see how I may change them to be more practical for successive semesters. For example, if I find that students are struggling with the syntax of a question, it will be reworded. If my students or I find a better answer than what I provide, I will modify my review materials to that end. These tasks sound elementary enough, but the course is so detailed that one has to get into the habit of making corrections on the spot or else it will be lost in the detail of preparing for another week's class. This is a task that you should do constantly—not just the first time you prepare to teach the course.

One primary method I use to assess my students is by administering a live, timed final examination. This two-hour exam tests my student's abilities in Westlaw, LexisNexis, and on free legal Web sites. It consists of a series of short questions that require research in different databases. It marks a chance for my students to apply everything that has been taught over the course of the semester. I have done this for a decade and find it's the ultimate, most practical way to assess the knowledge of my students.

I often start a class session with an introductory quick exercise based on a current legal action, such as a proposed or newly passed legislative bill or administrative regulation, or a recent trial court decision of interest. (Please see Appendix H for a few examples of this type of exercise.) There is usually a relevant story in every edition of major newspapers. I tell my students that they may use any means at their disposal to find the answer, to include the Internet, books, or any legal database. These introductory exercises serve as a platform to some of the most teachable moments of each class: Instead of *me* telling my students not to do something, or exclaiming in my lecture that they won't find certain material in the expected place immediately after becoming law, students have discovered this *on their own* by working through the exercises. These exercises teach students some basic, yet often unlearned, points of research. For instance, by requiring a public law number or docket number as part of the answer, students realize that oftentimes one cannot find the things required in practice from a general Google search. They are also finding out that, for instance, new legislation and new regulations do not automatically appear in the codes and they will sometimes need to find the law in its pre-codified form: It's still the law; it's just not where they are used to looking for it. Therefore, students come to realize that they need to know when and where to look for current information besides within the code databases. We discuss the exercise in class and students are asked to share how they found the answer. So another value to this type of exercise is that students are being taught by their peers.

The introductory exercises are also valuable in providing feedback as to the research preferences of my students. The reality is that students often use the free Internet. If students do not find the whole answer on the free Internet, I have pleasantly discovered that many of them have figured out that they need to take what they have found and move on to a more thorough source. I view this discovery with guarded optimism, in that if done correctly it serves the valuable purpose of either providing the answer for free or of providing enough information that a subsequent search in the pay databases will be much more accurate. However, caution must be taught as free Internet searching can be quite an exercise in futility and a time waster. So strict time limits should be considered whenever students might use the free Internet for legal research.

Another benefit of using introductory exercises (as well as in-class exercises) is that I am around to guide the students during the learning process. While trial-and-error is a good learning method, if you wait too long to step in to help students, it has the opposite effect of discouraging the learning process. By being close at hand, I bypass this issue at the initial and most critical period of development (contrast this with my description of the comprehensive take-home exercises described immediately below.).

I also rely on two take-home exercises that are designed to allow students to perform complete research projects by applying what they have learned in previous classes. These exercises allow me the ability to posit a fact pattern to which there is no clear answer, in an attempt to prepare students for what they are likely to encounter in the law firm setting. Students are made to compare and contrast documents in order to articulate both sides of an argument. To that end, these exercises give me a chance to relate the research to real-world writing assignments. I have found that without an anchoring writing component to my assignments, students are more likely to go through the motions in performing the research questions, which results in sloppy research and a lack of understanding as to the research process and its purpose. I am a firm believer that by incorporating some type of writing component, students are more likely to see the purpose of their research, and thus will produce a better product. I strive to keep the writing component as concise as possible for time considerations. In the past, I have used such writing components as short complaints, interoffice memorandums, and opinion letters.

I have students fill out timesheets as they perform the take-home exercises. I compile statistics on time spent and resources used (to include format), and compare them to the grades received. I then use this information to further hone my course. For a recent take-home assignment for one of my advanced legal research sections, those students starting the assignment with a print source had 12.8 percent higher grades than those who started online and spent fifty-five fewer minutes on the assignment. The average time on this assignment was about five hours, and those who started the project in the books saved nearly 20 percent of time on the assignment. Those who spent at least one-fourth of their research time in the books had 14.7 percent higher grades than those who spent less than one-fourth of their time using the books and spent twenty-nine fewer minutes on the assignment. These results reinforce my prior teaching on the typical research process for the inexperienced researchers, which involves starting with print-based secondary sources.

I use a pre-test and post-test to gauge learning throughout the semester. I compare the post-test scores to the pre-test scores as another method to assess student progress and to improve my course. I review the collective results and determine how to address deficiencies in successive semesters. The overall percentage increase also serves as a general indicator of my success. Of course, the level of success on a multiple-choice quiz is much more abstract than evaluating students when they are performing actual research, but it does serve a purpose. See Appendix I for sample pre-test/post-test questions.

I administer two or three quizzes during the semester. They may be graded or simply offered for extra credit. Either way has its benefits. Some of the quizzes are administered electronically, via my course Web site, which allows for easy statistical analysis: All but fill-in-the-blank questions are automatically graded and I can quickly see which questions need to be addressed to the class. I can also use the class average score for similar purposes. I administer e-polls, where students log onto the course Web site and anonymously answer a series of pre-drafted questions. I see the collective group vote and am able to instantly determine if more instruction is necessary. I have also developed games that sharpen research skills that are required to quickly and efficiently access the appropriate databases and that enable students to develop their search query formulation skills. In addition, we have just finished conducting our first boot camp review in an attempt to provide those students who are about to embark on summer clerkships with the necessary research skills to be an immediate asset to their employer.

I have structured my syllabus to reflect key learning components: Research strategy and query formulation, navigating retrieved documents, federal and California secondary source, case law/digest, legislative and administrative code, forms, court rules, legislative history, and citator services research. I actively assess these key points throughout the semester and often find it necessary to adjust for each section of students, as one section may understand a concept that the next section is having difficulty with. For instance, if results of a quick e-poll reveal that few students understood a lecture concept, I have the ability to remedy the situation on the spot. I consider this means of immediate group feedback to be highly useful—

especially combined with the fact that students are encouraged to vote due to the anonymity of their individual votes.

If you teach a course that is pass/fail instead of curved, then your responsibility to be occasional motivator expands from what it is in a graded course, as there is less of a fear factor involved with a pass/fail course. There are various means of motivation at your disposal. One means that can be employed from the beginning is choosing a high passing cutoff percentage—perhaps 75 percent. You can also keep students more engaged by assigning a few points to each in-class exercise and by having graded unannounced in-class quizzes. I have found that giving a live final exam, as described above, helps to hold attention throughout the course because students do not want to miss something that may help them on the live final exam.

As I administer a number of graded assignments and quizzes during the course of the semester, I have the opportunity to see what each student is having difficulty with when the assignments are being completed. This information allows me to know who needs a private meeting; or, if several students are having the same problem, it points to the need for more in-class training. If I feel the best course of action is to have a student or class redo a take-home assignment, then I will not hesitate to do so. I provide extensive notes on turned-in assignments. I also provide opportunities for students to perform extra practice assignments.

In the past, I have used practicum exercises as an additional means of motivation. These exercises consist of research questions that are to be answered within fifteen to twenty minutes, during class time, by individual students. Each student who participates in the practicum is required to return to the classroom within a certain time period and turn in their answers. Answers accounted for a certain percentage of the final grade. I found that even if the percentage was quite low, the exercises definitely captivated the attention of each student.

I also read every course evaluation. It is important to me that I continually seek improvements to my course in order to make it as practical and relevant as possible. I believe that an effective professor must be vigilant, watching each semester for issues that need to be addressed with each class section.

The Librarian's Role in Transitioning Students

The librarian's role in transitioning students is to best prepare them to conduct effective, practical legal research from their first day on the job. This involves instilling in them the basic research process and an ability to deftly conduct sundry legal research tasks in the online and print formats. As discussed earlier in this chapter (particularly in the Teaching Primary Research Skills section), new attorneys will likely be required to be familiar with secondary source research in both print and online formats as a means of becoming conversant with an unfamiliar area of law before searching through primary law. I also believe that we would do a disservice to our students if we do not prepare them for the range of possible research costs that they will likely face in the firm setting, as discussed previously.

My staff is always available for direction if a former student or law clerk contacts us. For example, our library has just completed the boot camp mentioned before in this article. Some attendees were former students. Other alumni e-mail, call, or simply come see us. In the future, we may directly involve local law firm librarians in the process for the purposes of improving student legal research abilities.

Key Areas of Expertise for Law School Librarians

The library staff manages a plethora of database, books, and other materials and often do not get adequate credit for navigating patrons through this maze of information, which often overwhelms the untrained researcher with information overload. Staff is also the database and book research experts who are more than willing to train patrons on every one of them. The databases and books themselves are important library resources. In particular, state and local legal resources get the most use, as students are likely to undertake legal jobs in the local area while enrolled in law school and would need access to those materials. In addition, many libraries allow their alumni—and sometimes the practicing bar—to use their print resources. Practitioners will most often use the local and state legal materials to complete their assignments. So it is essential that reference librarians be conversant with their state and local materials.

In addition to our primary role as educator, academic reference librarians must also conduct research for faculty, as well as being information providers, informal teacher via the provision of reference services to our various patron groups, technology facilitators, participators in the acquiring of relevant legal material for the library, and supervisors.

One cannot overlook the part that reference librarians play in the faculty's role of classroom educator and as publisher of educational material: We provide interlibrary loan and research services to all faculty, as well as current awareness services via RSS feeds and other push technology and from database highlights features. Many faculty view the provision of current awareness materials as being a critical component in their preparation of articles for publication, or for inclusion in their classroom lectures. Faculty members often do not have the time to acquire the information on their own, which makes the information even more valuable to them. Most of the Web sites that we depend on for legal current awareness news allow for the setup of RSS feeds, which push the selected information to our desktops: We choose the research parameters and then the documents that meet our criteria are automatically sent to our desktop at the designated day of the week. This saves the time of having to cull all of the information from the Web site every time we wish to provide updates to faculty members. The highlights feature, which is available on many Web sites or in many databases, collects the most important recent stories (often weekly). I simply e-mail the highlights page to the appropriate faculty members. Although the information is not "pushed" to me as with RSS feeds, all I have to do is go to one page on the Web site or to one place in the database to access the highlights. A lot of time is saved because I do not have to collect all of the documents before distributing them.

Librarians are in charge of making book and database purchasing decisions for the materials that are vital to our patrons. The process of selecting materials to purchase may take many forms, including assigning each librarian certain subjects, polling faculty for their input, passing out publisher catalogs to review (or using their online catalogs), reviewing various titles provided by acquisitions services, and reviewing current topical bibliographies. The roles of researcher, informal teacher, and technology facilitator are all components to formal classroom teaching.

As you have realized by now, technology plays a huge role in my classes. The academic law librarian must be adept in identifying and using multiple technologies. I use screenshot demonstrations, exercise reviews, lecture slides, and how-to programs that are shown in class via an LCD projector. Students in the back of the class may be just far enough from the projector screen to lose the requisite detail of the slides, so I also post sundry materials to my course Web site. Then students may view the presentation at their workstation while I am lecturing. All students will access documents that are posted to the course Web site when studying for the final exam. E-polling gives me a quick, anonymous way to determine if a lecture was understood. This is important, because I find that students are reluctant to let other students know that they do not understand a concept. Automatically graded online quizzes save me time and allow me to quickly assess tasks that need to be stressed again.

Students are able to take notes on their laptops and quickly pull up legal documents online while in class or while preparing for class. Unfortunately, advances in technology also allow students the ability to access materials during class that are not class related. I wholeheartedly believe that the average student has no idea how much their attention is diverted when multitasking. I realize that there is conflicting research on the effects of multitasking on classroom attention spans. However, I can speak from experience. The starkest example that I see regarding a lack of student attentiveness is when I am asked a question that I had specifically answered seconds earlier. This occurs enough of the time to conclude that there is more to it than students simply falling behind in their note taking. Although reasonable minds may differ as to the causes of classroom inattentiveness, I am convinced that student use of technology exacerbates what has been a long-standing educational issue.

Libraries and schools do not have an unlimited budget. This may affect the librarian's classroom technology usage at some schools. For instance, perhaps you may find that it is better to teach your class in the computer lab, as opposed to a regular classroom, but the lab does not have a mounted LCD projector. It may be cost prohibitive to purchase an LCD projector and have it mounted into the ceiling and secured. The alternative would be to have an AV cart wheeled in before every class. Perhaps your lab may not have been designed to serve as a classroom, and consequently there may not be adequate room for an AV cart. In that situation, you may need to rely on one of the popular class Web hosting services, which would enable faculty to upload presentations before class.

Budgetary issues may arise more often if your school has a sudden jump in enrollment, which may result in an unexpected shortage of database or software user licenses. In this instance, it would be beneficial to have cushion in the budget that would allow for the ability to pay for more licenses. Setting up secure, remote access (VPN) may also be an issue that could require extra money and staffing.

There are seven areas of expertise that I believe are of key importance for all law school reference librarians. A mastery of many of these areas enhances classroom effectiveness. Here is my list of key areas of expertise:

1) *Knowledge of a plethora of technology*

> Why: Students will be using it all. You have to remain relevant.
> How to acquire: Read and practice
> Resources required: Library may purchase relevant magazine subscriptions

2) *Be adept at Web searching and searching your online library catalog*

> Why: To produce work product and to become efficient at reference services
> How to acquire: Read about how various search engines work; practice; find out what students use
> Resources required: Library may purchase relevant magazine subscriptions

3) *Knowledge of Web editing software and electronic newsletter software*

Why: To maintain library Web pages and produce newsletter
How to acquire: Attend formal or informal training sessions; read and practice
Resources required: Library may purchase relevant software

4) *Knowledge of word processing programs and spreadsheets*

Why: To produce quality work product
How to acquire: Read and practice
Resources required: Library may purchase relevant magazine subscriptions or books

5) *Knowledge of major publishers and materials available in major legal subject areas*

Why: To be able to help the library in its collection development function; to become better at providing reference and research services
How to acquire: Review published catalogs; browse library stacks; ask area experts for the most important titles; look at bibliographies provided within major area treatises or from other libraries

6) *Knowledge of basic legal research*

Why: To teach and to provide reference services
How to acquire: Review legal research books/hornbooks; audit a legal research and an advanced legal research course; ask questions of your supervisor or other knowledgeable librarians; prepare a legal research course; teach

7) *Personnel management*

Why: You may very well be asked to supervise staff or students
How to acquire: Classes or seminars; ask questions; observe how supervisors interact with subordinates while at work; ask to help supervise student workers

Patrick Meyer is an associate library director and adjunct professor of law at Thomas Jefferson School of Law. He has taught MCLE courses and developed advanced legal research courses. Professor Meyer has taught extensively in the past ten years.

Professor Meyer is in charge of the public services department of the library. In addition to being the associate library director, he also teaches two sections of advanced legal research each semester and is heavily involved in the research and use of classroom technology.

Professor Meyer is the immediate past president of the Southern California Association of Law Libraries (SCALL), a group of about 400 law librarians. SCALL is a chapter of the American Association of Law Libraries. Professor Meyer is also a member of the ThomsonWest Legal Research and Writing Advisory Board.

Professor Meyer received his J.D. from Washburn University School of Law, his M.L.S. from Syracuse University, and his M.S. in mass communications, with emphasis in public relations, from Kansas State University.

The Roles and Status of the Academic Law Library Director

Barbara Bintliff

Nicholas Rosenbaum Professor of Law and Director,
William A. Wise Law Library
University of Colorado at Boulder

ASPATORE

An academic law library director plays several key roles in the law school. One role is that of the CEO of a small business.[1] As such, the director has many responsibilities—dealing with both professional and clerical personnel (advertising and recruiting, hiring, training, evaluating, compensating, promoting, and terminating) and building a management team; overseeing the day-to-day library operation; developing missions and goals, policies, business plans, and strategic directions; managing budgets; marketing; and ensuring compliance with safety regulations, all while overseeing large, technologically sophisticated facilities. The law library director is a leader who provides strategic thinking for her enterprise.

The law library director also is a middle manager in the law school and university hierarchy. In addition to having a staff that reports to them, law librarians report to a dean, who in turn reports to a provost or other university officer. Law library directors face the same challenges as other middle managers—following and leading from the middle. Law library directors must interpret and implement law school and university policies and rules; compete for resources with other departments; and engage in operational thinking as they balance the conflicting demands of their own department with the larger organization's. Like other middle managers, law librarians prepare for their roles by completing management and administration classes in library school and, most typically, working their way through the ranks, gaining experience in business operations along the way.

Managing a Law School Library

Librarianship has traditionally focused on the evaluation, organization, and dissemination of information, and library management directed those activities. Until recently, however, that meant that librarians primarily dealt

---

[1] Law library budgets are substantial, staffs are a mix of professional and clerical workers with a wide range of duties, and facilities serve multiple purposes (research facility, computer lab, instructional space, individual and group study areas, etc.). The average law library spent $2,569,938 in 2005-2006. The average staff size was 19.8 FTE, not including student assistants. American Bar Association, Section on Legal Education and Admissions to the Bar, Law Library Comprehensive Statistical Table Data From Fall 2006 Annual Questionnaire, items 24.2 "FTE library staff" and 51 "total spent," (ABA: Chicago, IL, 2007).

with books and microfiche and the occasional computer file or archival collection. Librarianship still focuses on the evaluation, organization, and dissemination of information, but those processes are far different today and require different skills and knowledge. Subscriptions to electronic resources, databases developed internally to customized expectations, and the universe of Internet-based sources complement tangible library collections and raise many new management issues.

For example, the physical library facility undergoes constant transformation, as different mixes of technology and electronic and print resources evolve. As the law school curriculum changes and students need to use library resources differently, the library's physical space may change from emphasizing smaller, individual study areas to larger, more open and flexible work spaces and study rooms where people can sit together and talk. Technology is now available freely, throughout the library, moving from the locked rooms of previous years.

Human resource management is another important role of the academic law library director, and one that requires changed thinking from previous years. For example, it is increasingly important to find staff members who are flexible and have good interpersonal skills. In the past, for example, library wisdom was that, when you hired a technical services librarian it did not matter if he or she had good social skills and could communicate well as long as the books were ordered, cataloged, and classified correctly and quickly. Similarly, public service librarians often were hired primarily for their good people skills and research knowledge, rather than their attention to business detail or follow-up abilities; their work with the library's clientele required social skills and communications. However, libraries now need all staff to have well-developed interpersonal and collaborative skills and knowledge of a range of library issues in addition to their subject specialties. Reference librarians collaborate with catalogers on the development of user-friendly catalog interfaces and the transition from a catalog to a research portal. To ease and speed the transition, librarians have to understand how library users use those portals, and how technicians develop them. Recruiting and managing individuals with several skill sets challenges today's law library director.

Like other middle managers, law library directors develop and implement budgets. The law library director identifies library needs, researches and assigns costs, and submits a budget request to the law school dean that explains each item. Budget requests typically must fit within a strategic plan or other law school or university framework. The constantly changing technology landscape makes budget preparation almost a moving target, but the importance of library technological offerings to the law school faculty and staff cannot be overestimated. Identifying and justifying needs for electronic information resources, updated management applications, hardware upgrades, and information management staff, in addition to all other library needs, requires foresight and nimbleness in a law library director.

In addition to managing space, people, and budgets, today's law librarians also play a role in understanding and implementing new technologies. The academic law library director who can keep abreast of developments in all law school technologies and understand their application in legal education is rare, but the accomplished director can oversee and direct those whose job it is to do so. Indeed, this is an important role for law library directors, as technology shapes almost everything the modern law library does. Law school librarians deliver information by means of the most appropriate, efficient, and effective technology. They teach the use of technologies and electronic resources. Law libraries repackage and provide information in new and different forms, such as creating customized databases for professors, and sponsoring blogs that involve student contributors.

Further, law libraries are frequently the technology-leaders in the law school. Libraries were usually the first program in a law school to adopt computerized management systems, develop electronic databases, and use e-mail for daily communications. Librarians routinely used technology in teaching and information delivery before classroom faculty. Their knowledge and long experience with technology—its applications, the rate at which it changes, storage and maintenance requirements, staffing, etc.—make librarians important players in the law school technology program.

Meeting Expectations

Students and professors, the law school library's primary clientele, have many expectations of a law school library these days. Students expect the library to be an absolutely quiet study space, and yet a place where they can collaborate. They want all the information imaginable at their fingertips, and they want someone readily available to show them how to use that information. Expectations on the part of students have escalated rapidly in recent years, and law librarians have pushed to meet those expectations.

New library services, approved and managed by the library director, meet and exceed these student expectations. Law libraries offer multipurpose facilities that meet many student work needs. They provide training and instruction in print and electronic formats. The instruction may be through published research guides, one-on-one, in the classroom, via podcast, on the Web, with avatars in SecondLife, or in a variety of other ways. Librarians are adept innovators, balancing student needs, staff abilities, technological functions, facilities, and budgets to meet expectations.

Faculty members, on the other hand, do not care as much about the library's physical space or most of its instructional programs, in large part because of the growing emphasis placed on information delivery to faculty desktops. Law librarians have worked hard to make information delivery seamless to faculty, and to anticipate faculty's legal information needs. Most faculty now expect that information will be on their desks before they even know they need it. Librarians provide instruction to faculty informally, when needed or requested, making it easy for faculty to research from home or office. Law librarians have inadvertently shielded the faculty from the library in many cases, and faculty do not realize what it takes to make this amazing delivery of information and resources possible.

This consequence points out a common shortcoming in library management, which is educating faculty (and administration) on the services and resulting needs of the law library. The faculty should be the law library's biggest supporters, especially at budget-time, and they will advocate for the library if they understand what personnel and resources are needed to support class preparation and research. If faculty do not understand the law library's resource needs, however, they will not back up library requests.

Many law library directors are confronting this reality in a variety of ways, especially by using marketing techniques ranging from annual reports and presentations at faculty meetings to informal conversations in the elevators and hallways.

Identifying and Evaluating Law School Requirements for Library Resources

In order to determine demand for the library's services and resources, law school librarians pay close attention to what information is requested and by whom; curricular developments; faculty research needs; and student classroom and seminar requirements. Surveys and questionnaires are developed and administered. Current developments in librarianship and related service fields are monitored for new services or programs that might be implemented. Law library directors realize the importance of meeting the changing needs of the law library's clientele, and are always on the lookout for something new to try.

For example, law librarians work hard to anticipate resource demands before new classes meet and before faculty become engrossed in a new project. When curricular discussions are held in faculty meetings, law library directors routinely describe the impact on the library and its budget of adding a new course or program or hiring a faculty member with a research focus that differs from that of existing faculty. As faculty develop their research agendas, law librarians meet with them and identify resource needs. A recurring question is, "What do we have in our collection that supports that effort?" Law librarians track faculty information requirements, often developing in-house databases, spreadsheets, or profiles. Using this information, the librarians evaluate potential new resources, compare them with existing resources, and confer with the individual faculty members to assure the best coverage of the subject. Academic law libraries must be proactive, now and for the future, in identifying and meeting their clientele's needs, and thereby remaining relevant in a fast-changing information world.

Yes, the academic law library director is a businessperson, both a small business CEO and a middle manager. Her responsibilities are many and her days are busy. Why, then, should the academic status of the academic law library director be an issue? The answer lies in both the historical development of the position and in the unique role of the academic law library in the education of law students.

Intellectual Leadership

Like modern librarianship generally, law librarians can trace their history to the late 1800s. The profession of law librarianship grew up with the modern law school. As noted in the recent Carnegie Foundation study, law students were "introduced by their professors to legal research,"[2] beginning around the 1870s, instruction made necessary by the "fast-expanding mass"[3] of American legal materials. Before long, those professors who had been teaching legal research to their students evolved into law librarians, not only teaching students the intricacies of legal research but also managing the rapidly growing legal information resources. The professors retained their faculty status and titles, while increasingly specializing in law librarianship.

A member of the teaching faculty was appointed to oversee the library and ensure the availability of the necessary books and periodicals for the law school's educational program because that person's experience *as a faculty member* was considered essential to providing the best library possible for the law students and faculty. Today's law library is infinitely more complex than that of years' past, making professional training and experience in librarianship, as well as law, required for the effective oversight of the law library. But the law library director of today continues in the role of her predecessors, ensuring that the legal information resources necessary for first year legal research and writing courses, seminar papers, all other law school courses, and faculty scholarship are available, appropriate, and accessible. Her experience as a faculty member remains key to the most effective provision of library services.

Academic law librarians have been members of the law school faculty, with full faculty status and tenure, since their beginnings in the law school classroom. The American Bar Association (ABA), legal education's accrediting body, and the Association of American Law Schools (AALS),

---

[2] William M. Sullivan, et al., Educating Lawyers: Preparation for the Profession of Law, at 6. (John Wiley, San Francisco: 2007).
[3] Id.

the scholarly society for law schools, recognize the essential role of law library directors in their respective rules. For example, faculty status and tenure for the academic law library director are required by the ABA under standard 603(d), which says that "except in extraordinary circumstances" a director shall hold a law faculty appointment.[4] The AALS has a similar requirement that says that the director of the law school library should have both a legal and library education, and should be a "full participating member of the faculty."[5] There is no way to be a full participating member of the faculty without having full faculty status and the job security afforded by tenure.

To think, then, of an academic law library director as purely a businessperson, an academic administrator, is to misunderstand the purpose of the law library itself. The library is not just a "function" to be managed. The library is an essential part of the law school's educational program and the permanent intellectual resource of the law school. The law library director provides intellectual leadership for the law school, in the present and for the future, as she directs the development of this key resource.

AALS' bylaws describe the library as "an integral part of the law school"[6] that is to be "organized and administered to perform its educational function."[7] The ABA's Standards call for a law library that is "an active and responsive force in the educational life of the law school."[8] The ABA recognizes that legal research is one of the fundamental skills necessary to participate effectively in the legal profession; legal research instruction, a primary library service, is one of the fields of instruction the ABA *requires* a law school to offer as part of its educational program.

---

[4] ABA Standard 603(d) appears in Appendix A.

[5] AALS ECR 6-8.6 appears in Appendix B.

[6] Association of American Law Schools, Bylaws, Library, Sec. 6.8 (b) (AALS: Washington, D.C. 2007). Available at http://www.aals.org/about_handbook_bylaws.php.

[7] Id.

[8] American Bar Association Section on Legal Education and Admissions to the Bar, Standards for Approval of Law Schools, Standard 601 (ABA: Chicago, IL, 2007). Available at http://www.abanet.org/legaled/standards/20072008StandardsWebContent/Chapter%206.pdf,

As a member of the faculty, the law library director understands fully the issues facing the law school and has a role in addressing them. Recognizing him or her as anything but a faculty member shortchanges the school's students and handicaps its faculty by not giving them the best library possible.

There are, in fact, four main reasons that the academic law library director must have full faculty status and tenure. These reasons are that:

1. The law library is the permanent intellectual resource of the law school.
2. Academic freedom is essential to the provision of library resources and services.
3. Scholarship on topics related to law librarianship is critical to the law school program.
4. Ensuring strong leadership of the law library requires appropriate status and incentives for law library directors.

Each reason is sufficient to merit faculty status, as explained below.

1. The Law Library is the permanent intellectual resource of the law school.

The law library director of today ensures that the legal information resources necessary for first year legal research and writing courses, seminar papers, and all other law school courses, and for faculty research and scholarship, are available, appropriate, and accessible. The growth of electronic resources has complicated the job. It hasn't changed what law library directors do, but it has changed how it is done. The law library director must still apply her knowledge of law school educational goals, faculty research interests, the curriculum, and student needs to the development of the library's collections and programs. Her experience *as a faculty member* remains key to the most effective provision of library services.

2. Academic freedom is essential to the provision of library resources and services.

The American university is a unique organization in that its governance is shared by its administration and a select group of its employees, the faculty, with clear delegation of duties to each. Faculty are charged with the responsibility to develop and oversee curricular and academic matters, and to engage in research and scholarship that expands knowledge. Sometimes faculty decisions are controversial. Endorsing a new method of teaching, for example by requiring more experiential learning and less in-class time, can lead to questions about effective use of time and resources, although learning by doing is becoming commonplace in today's universities. Developing curricula in newer fields, for example, gender studies or ethnic studies, may challenge traditional thinking. Providing information resources to support new initiatives is equally controversial, as librarians well know.

Academic freedom protects faculty as they make academic decisions and librarians as they acquire materials to implement the decisions. Tenure allows faculty to exercise their academic freedom without fear of reprisal from university administrators or the public. Law library directors, like all faculty, need and deserve the protections of academic freedom and tenure:

- If the classroom faculty member deserves protection in the selection of books and readings, so does the librarian faculty member in developing the library's collection, including the selection of resources covering multiple viewpoints, controversial topics, and emerging subjects.

- If the classroom faculty member deserves protection in discussing and teaching competing theories and ideologies and philosophies, so does the librarian faculty member in helping students use resources from a range of viewpoints.

- If the classroom faculty member deserves protection in research and writing, the librarian faculty member deserves protection in producing finding aids, catalogs, and pathfinders for the library's patrons, in addition to deserving academic freedom for his or her own scholarly pursuits.

- If the classroom faculty member's expertise is needed in the shared governance of the law school, so is the librarian faculty member's, whose focus is on the common good of all students and faculty and complements the specialized interests of individual classroom faculty.

Academic freedom protects a faculty member's scholarship, teaching, and intellectual pursuits of all kinds. Academic freedom is characterized by openness, and by dialog, consensus, and vote. Academic freedom encourages a wider rather than a narrower range of views in teaching, in research, and in faculty governance. Law library directors bring a "big picture" to this dialog. Their experience in providing for the legal information needs of the entire law school community brings a breadth to the conversation that no other single faculty member can provide, and is indispensable if faculty governance is to be well reasoned.

3. Scholarship on topics related to law librarianship is critical to the law school program.

A component of faculty status is the requirement that faculty members produce scholarship and publish in their field of expertise. Law librarianship has a rich and vital tradition of scholarship. Law librarians have traditionally focused their scholarship on topics such as legal research methods, pedagogy, and philosophy, and the organization and management of legal information resources. Significant research tools, suggested methodologies, and extensive bibliographies, produced by law librarians, are in use in legal writing and research programs nationwide. It is difficult to imagine adequate legal research instruction, a fundamental skill, without the scholarly contributions of law librarians. Similarly, without the current and historical scholarship on legal research and legal resources, much of the research foundation for faculty writing would be almost impossible.

There are those who raise the scholarship of librarianship as an objection to librarian faculty status and tenure, charging that librarians' scholarship is not relevant to legal education, and has not remained relevant, as the legal field has changed. This is flat wrong. Traditional librarian scholarship provides the foundation for teaching legal research and explaining sophisticated resources and methods. Further, many law library directors are expanding their research to include investigations into the impact of the Internet and electronic resources on legal research and legal thinking. They are exploring issues of authentication and preservation of legal documents that exist only in electronic format, and question the extent of copyright protections for essential educational materials. These are important topics that directly affect legal education.

The conclusions and solutions in this research are strengthened by the experience of the law library director as both businessperson and academician. Like the other subject specialists hired by the law school, whether in intellectual property or securities or affordable housing or evidence or social justice or in any of the extraordinary range of fields of inquiry pursued by law faculty, the law library director's scholarship contributes to the expansion of knowledge and the law school's mission.

Within our universities, we have found ways to extend faculty status and tenure to dancers and physicists, engineers and linguists, journalists and sculptors. We know how to evaluate many kinds of scholarship and creative works. Within our law schools, we have collectively agreed to evaluate and tenure doctrinal scholars, post-modernist legal philosophers, and storytellers. We promote and tenure those who explore corporate mergers and acquisitions as well as those who propose deconstruction of our legal system. Scholarship on topics related to legal research and information management fit squarely within the milieu of academic pursuits already accepted by universities nationwide, and is equally worthy of supporting faculty status and a grant of tenure.

4. Ensuring strong leadership of the law library requires appropriate status and incentives for law library directors.

Law libraries are centers of collaborative learning and of self-directed study. They are the repository for the scholarly record of the law and portals to a worldwide body of knowledge. Law libraries are where law students go when they want to "get serious" about their study. Law libraries are a physical gathering place for students and the heart of the law school community. Use of the library and its resources, by students and faculty, is increasing each year, especially as the mix of print and electronic formats becomes more complementary and sophisticated, and as more help from librarians is needed in using the resources. The law library is an irreplaceable asset to the educational and scholarly mission of the law school. This complex organization requires significant knowledge, leadership abilities, and management skills of its director.

There is a shortage of qualified librarians today, in law libraries and in the profession in general. Filling jobs at all levels, and in all specialties, has been difficult for several years. The federal government, recognizing the shortage and realizing that librarianship is absolutely critical to the nation's education infrastructure, made $10 million in grants available in 2003 and $21 million in 2004 to recruit and educate a new generation of librarians.[9] To attract the strongest candidates to law librarianship, and especially to the law library director's position, law schools must offer appropriate incentives, which include faculty status and the opportunity to earn tenure.

Librarians with faculty status who have earned tenure through the same processes as classroom faculty have a greater understanding of faculty expectations and needs, and are in a better position to enhance the quality of research, teaching, and service in their respective schools. Without faculty status and the opportunity to gain tenure, those interested in law librarianship will turn to other careers, further reducing the field of qualified professionals for this key law school role. It is not in the best interests of the law faculty, the law students, or the law school to have law library directors who are disconnected from scholarship, governance, or the tenure process.

Some on the business side of universities want to do away with faculty status and tenure for librarians. They claim that librarians have no faculty duties and do not deserve faculty status or tenure. In truth, they would prefer no long-term commitment to any individual—faculty or not—in order to maximize the institution's budgetary and personnel flexibility; they would eliminate tenure for everyone. Librarians are often only the first on the list when proposals to eliminate faculty status and tenure are developed. These are purely economic arguments, not based on the role of the academic law librarian but rather on a desire to hire and fire academic employees at will.

Numerous professional organizations and universities dispute these claims and protest the elimination of librarian faculty status, pointing out the vital roles played by librarians in teaching and research. The American Association of University Professors, which promulgated the standard

---

[9] See, e.g., http://www.whitehouse.gov/firstlady/initiatives/recruitmentandeducation.html

statement supporting faculty status and tenure for classroom faculty,[10] collaborated with the Association of College and Research Librarians to produce a clear statement on faculty status for librarians.[11] Many colleges and universities around the country offer faculty status to their librarians. Serious researchers and scholars support librarian faculty status and tenure because they recognize the educational contributions of librarians.

Conclusion

The academic law library director fills many roles in the law school. She is a manager, and oversees the largest academic program in the law school besides the classroom curriculum. And she is a teacher, instructing students in the use, evaluation, organization, and assessment of legal information resources. The law library is the permanent intellectual resource of the law school, outlasting even the longest-tenured faculty member (or librarian). Without a law library, no law school could offer its educational program, fulfill its research mission, or provide outreach services to the bar, the bench, or the public. Teaching, research, and service—the three prongs of any educational institution's mission, including a law school's—are unreachable without the law library.

Law library directors are key members of the educational enterprise. Their decisions shape the present and future of the legal education offered by the law school, and guide the research and scholarship of generations of faculty. They must couple their business acumen with the in-depth knowledge of the educational enterprise gained through participation in that enterprise as a faculty member. The full participation of the law library director in law school activities and governance best determines whether the requirements of the ABA accreditation standards are met and whether the library is well managed and responsive to its clientele.

---

[10] American Association of University Professors, Statement of Principles on Academic Freedom and Tenure, available at
http://www.aaup.org/AAUP/pubsres/policydocs/contents/1940statement.htm
[11] Association of College and Research Libraries, Joint Statement on Faculty Status of College and University Librarians, appears in Appendix J.

Barbara Bintliff is a Nicholas Rosenbaum professor of law and director at William A. Wise Law Library, University of Colorado at Boulder. She received her J.D. from the University of Washington and her M.L.L. from the University of Washington.

Dedication: *This chapter is dedicated to the generations of academic law library directors who created a profession vital to the success of law schools, integral to the education of lawyers, and challenging to its practitioners.*

Working with Students and Faculty in the Research Process

Barbara Glennan

Assistant Director for Electronic and Outreach Services

California Western School of Law

ASPATORE

Meeting the Challenges of a Changing Role

There are various types of librarians within a law school, and those who primarily serve in a public service function, as I do, are typically much more handson with the students. We spend a great deal of our time demonstrating how to access and use library materials, making our students aware of any new resources that are available, especially the latest electronic resources.

In recent years, we have found that library reference statistics have gone down a bit, but we also find that there is a greater demand for formal and informal instruction by librarians. Our public services librarians are taking on the role of a guest lecturer or adjunct professor. Our school offers an advanced legal research class, an international legal research class, and may soon be offering a business research class—all taught by librarians. We have also been providing more informal instruction to faculty members, which is a beneficial trend because it gets the word out about what librarians know, and it helps us to integrate our skills into the organization, which is a win-win situation for both the library and the institution.

The way in which people access information by using the Internet has changed the culture of research to some extent, and librarians are often the first people within a law school to know about or adopt new research technologies, or to work with students who have already adopted the technologies. Therefore, we are the in-house experts on research technology, and faculty members (as well as students) are looking to us to teach them what we know, as opposed to just asking us for help in answering reference questions.

This new emphasis on the librarian's teaching role has created some new challenges in that while in-person reference questions have gone down a bit, the reference desk itself is still an important first point of contact for many of our patrons. Therefore, we need to be able to manage our time in such a way that we are able to have time away from the reference desk to prepare for lectures or other projects.

Teaching Legal Research Skills

In our role as educator, the law school librarian's primary task is to assist law students in developing legal research skills. We work with the legal skills instructors in their teaching of first year students about the basic print and electronic legal resources. Once we get to the advanced level we try to fill in any holes in their education with respect to information that they may not have already obtained from their basic legal research skills classes: this could range from Westlaw/Lexis to practice guides to the latest Web 2.0 trends. We may need to explain basic concepts such as the difference between the Code of Federal Regulations (CFR) and the U.S. Code, or what a session law is. In our advanced research classes, we teach students the various ways to access information using different publishers and formats. We also explain what information you can get for free and what you have to pay for, in order to enhance the student's awareness of cost-effectiveness research practices.

It is always important for law students to understand the nature of the information they are accessing, because this will not change, but the format and the interfaces of various information sources will change over time. We go over the difference between primary law and secondary (commentary) resources and the "weight" or authority that should be given to various sources. For example, a law review article written by a judge or a professor may have more "weight" than an article on the same topic written by a student, even though the student-written article may be clearer and easier to understand. It is important to take all of these factors into account when researching. We try to teach our students how to analyze the nature of the information they are obtaining through the research process, because if they do not know how to do that properly, the quality of whatever it is they are trying to produce (a legal memo, for example) will not be as good. From there we go into the nuances of the different types of formats and publications available in legal materials.

At the same time, I have found that there are some aspects of the research process that you cannot teach; rather, students must often learn from hands-on experience. When teaching a class, I view myself as someone who gives the students the basic data about a resource, i.e., how to use it, what it contains, etc, but I also need to make sure that they are given the opportunity to apply this knowledge through experiencing the research process for themselves. I have found that exercises (fact patterns to be researched in particular resources) are a good way of doing this. It provides "guided experience" for those students who are just beginning to learn about a resource or the research process, and can provide validation for those with some experience. Students usually find there is almost always more than one way to research a particular issue—there is no single path. I find the process of lecture and guided exercises develops both a student's skills and their confidence. Armed with this knowledge and experience, students can then start teaching themselves about the topic they are researching and the materials that they find. Once they get the "hang" of the research process, they will be able to evaluate information on their own, which is an essential skill for clerking or practicing law.

Students who are engaged in a research exercise often have various anxieties with respect to the information that they need to obtain, or the format that they need to use may seem intimidating. At the same time, they are often dealing with a time crunch in relation to their other work. All of these factors often make learning the research process extremely challenging. This is one way the guided research exercises are valuable, as they provide a frame of reference for students to use when they are in a "real-life" situation. If a student does not seem to understand some of the basics, you can deduct points in order to give them an incentive to work harder, or you can allow them to repeat an exercise. I have found that this is a very effective process, because as students become more experienced and confident they will find that important information will start sinking in.

Helping Students Transition from Law School to Law Firm

Over the years, I have had many students come back after graduation and tell me that they were more confident once they began clerking or practicing law because of the research skills they learned in the advanced legal research course. Conversely, I have known other students who did not receive that kind of research skill training, and did not feel as capable in their research tasks once they began to practice after graduation. Therefore, teaching students these valuable research skills gives them the knowledge and confidence that they need so that they can hit the ground running when they begin their careers.

Our library has just begun conducting brown bag lunch lectures for students about "transitioning to practice." Our first topic was practice resources in two of the states (outside of California) that many of our graduates ultimately practice in. We discussed how to get information on taking the bar exam and bar review courses in those states; resources for finding a job; as well as an overview of the unique practice materials that are used by attorneys in those states. This topic was received well by students and will be repeated in the future.

The Role of Technology in Legal Research Education

Web links to electronic resources via the law library Website are among the most important resources for a law school library these days. Faculty and students are taking advantage of the library's electronic resources from wherever they may be: on campus, at home, or out of town. In addition to subscribed resources, librarians have also created online research guides and tutorials. These guides include subject guides to assist those researching specific topics (i.e., "elder law") as well as tutorials on how to use specific tools, for example, "how to use a digest."

Other forms of technology that are helpful to both teachers and students include class Web sites that may include assignments, a syllabus, handouts, presentation slides, and links to relevant resources. The library provides access to these sources via a student's laptop (through the wired or wireless network) or via our student computer lab computers.

Some people like learning about the latest research technologies while others are afraid of them. One can be a competent researcher using only selected technologies. As stated before, there is no "one" path to finding most materials, so a combination of online and print is acceptable, and sometimes preferable. However, there are a few technologies that every researcher must learn. A research must know how to search the Internet (i.e., use Google "Advanced Search" menus), know how to use e-mail, and know how to update the information (particularly primary law such as codes and case law) they find. Electronic citators (such as KeyCite or Shepards), are the best way to update case law and (in the case of KeyCite) may be able to update codes.

At the same time, the use of technology in teaching has to be focused on student learning. A classic problem nationwide is that many students are inclined to play with their laptop computers in the classroom instead of listening to a lecture, and as a result, some professors and schools have banned laptops and/or network access from their classrooms, over the protests of their students. Unfortunately, in such instances, technology can be a problem. If a laptop becomes a distraction and/or actually gets in the way of learning or communicating with the student, faculty and school administration may want to control its use. Another area where technology may be seen as going too far is in recording or broadcasting classroom lectures. It can be quite helpful for students to view recorded lectures so that they can review the materials. However, there are many who feel that providing an entire law class online would create a loss of interaction between students and between the students and the professor, to the detriment to the learning process. As new more interactive forms of technology are developed and implemented in the classroom, this balance between educational goals and technological convenience may be easier to manage.

Key Library Resources

The people who work in a library—its librarians—are its most valuable resources, because all of our materials would be of no use unless our librarians told our patrons about them, and showed them how to use those resources. Librarians do this in a number of ways. We organize, classify, provide access, answer reference questions, guest lecture, create user guides, as well as teach entire courses on research.

Electronic materials are certainly demanding a larger part of our attention these days. I have direct responsibility for our library Web site, which provides links to many of our electronic resources. I am also part of the group that helps to choose those resources. We are currently implementing a new electronic management system (ERM) which will enable us to provide links to many of our electronic resources through our catalog, help keep links updated, and help us organize the materials (licenses and other information) related to the resource. We are just beginning to learn what our ERM can do; the ability to track information associated with electronic resources has been sorely needed for some time.

Many of our best print resources, such as multi-volume treatises and practice guides, are now available in electronic format. This is often (but not always) a better way to access, as anyone on campus has access at the same time. However, the usability of the resource's interface is sometimes poorly thought out, making it difficult to use. In addition, print resources are still important. Not everything is in electronic format, and even if it is, it may be more cost effective (for example, in a law firm) to access materials initially in print format, and then update with electronic resources. This is because some resources (such as Westlaw/Lexis) may charge by the time spent online. In addition, not everyone is a proficient online researcher; some may work more efficiently in print. Therefore, a law school library must have all of its primary research materials available in various formats for educational and research purposes, depending on how they can best support the curriculum.

Collaborative Practices for Leveraging Resources

Reference librarians often do guest lectures for our faculty. They may hand us a syllabus or some exercises and say, "I want my students to be able to do this type of project—what does the library have to offer to help them?" We will then tailor a lecture for the students in which we explain the different resources that our library provides to help them with their classes. We will try to make these lectures as interactive as possible. The librarians keep track of what classes are being offered and where our curriculum is concentrated in order to select materials that support it. We will often send trials of new databases to faculty for review, and requests by faculty for materials to support their teaching or research are given high priority.

We have recently begun hosting a once a month "research lunch" in which the librarians or outside speakers cover important research or educational technology topics during a lunchtime gathering. The idea is to keep our faculty updated about the latest trends in the field. We also help them keep up their skills by bringing in Lexis or Westlaw representatives. These gatherings have been well received and help the library keep better connected with the research needs of the faculty.

The increased use of distance and online learning in legal education is perhaps inevitable, and it is important to determine how to regulate it. Our school has offered a few experimental online learning courses, and the library had input into creating and implementing guidelines for those courses.

The process of purchasing electronic materials is handled by a library committee called the Electronic Resources Working Group (ERWG), in a collaborative process involving both our public services and tech services people, who meet on a regular basis in order to decide which electronic materials to buy. Our library has a collection development checklist that we go through in order to decide which resources would best support the curriculum, and which are most cost effective. This collaborative approach to acquisitions is very helpful in that it educates both the public and technical services areas of the library about what is useful for our institution. Our ERM will be especially helpful to this group as we are hoping it will help us keep track of details on a specific system, and give us all an easy way to track and access this data.

Developing Curriculum in Key Practice Areas

Our public services librarians recently started developing a business research class (with the oversight of the library director). We decided to offer business research after surveying students on what topic areas they felt they lacked knowledge of research processes and sources. We may add other research areas as the school's curriculum or students' interests change. Our goal is to offer research courses that our students have interest in and would be most helpful to them in their law school or future practice careers.

In my role as part of our library's public services group, I also work with our public services librarians to create research guides for our students and faculty. We have developed some informative legal skills and resources guides that many of our legal skills professors really like and have put them on our Website.

The curriculum for lectures and classes on research topics has to be updated regularly. I have taught advanced legal research for over twelve years, and before giving a lecture I will always go over its content to ensure that it is completely up to date. Recently new librarians have joined our staff and are educating us with the latest trends and new ideas, which they use to develop their own classes. This has inspired me to try to totally reinvent my syllabus, and I'm in the midst of this process right now.

Key Areas of Expertise for the Law School Librarian

In many cases, a law school librarian's role expands beyond the library or the classroom. One of the more enjoyable aspects of a librarian's career path is the variety that it can offer. For example, many librarians are involved in management. This can require knowledge of many things including employment law, organizational structure, public relations, and sometimes heating and air conditioning! Some librarians are involved in management of computer resources and networks (IT), as this relates to the distribution of information throughout an organization. Some may be required to know a little about all of the above in order to fulfill the requirements of their particular position.

For example, I currently work with another colleague and two other departments on campus in developing educational technology. This is a new job duty and we are working out ways in which we can be most useful to our organization. The current project in this area is investigating and learning about digital class recording systems, and determining what system would work best for our campus. I also oversee the students' computer lab with the assistance of 1.5 full-time technicians. This involves knowledge of hardware and software at both the desktop and network level. We work with students to assist them in connecting their laptops to the network, and make sure that our lab contains up-to-date hardware as well as software needed to support the students attending classes here.

Today's law school librarian needs to have a great deal of expertise in areas outside the standard library school curriculum. Of course, you need to understand legal resources—what they are and what they do—but I also recommend at least a knowledge of basic computer and networking operation, including operating systems as well the types of software in the Microsoft Office Suite: PowerPoint, Excel spreadsheet, and word processing. Interpersonal skills are key for working with patrons, teaching, and networking inside and outside the library. A basic knowledge of management practices and training is useful for every librarian, even if you are not in a management position, because it helps you to understand your manager's priorities. Public relations skills are also useful as they help when a librarian needs to communicate with various constituencies including faculty, administrators, and outside vendors, which can at times be challenging if not intimidating.

Since we work with information resources—especially electronic resources—it is helpful for a librarian to have a basic knowledge of copyright. From time to time, a professor will ask me to send them certain articles in a law journal so that they can in turn send them to their students, but the copyright laws may prohibit this. This also comes up in relation to student downloads of audio and video materials. In addition, understanding basic contract and licensing concepts is important when subscribing to electronic resources.

Time Management Techniques and Benchmarking Performance

I don't pretend to be a role model for time management; I am always looking for ways to improve in this area. However, one thing I learned from taking a class on the topic some years ago is to keep only one calendar. I am currently using Outlook, as it is provided by my employer, and I have the same system on my home computer. I flag my e-mail notices for later attention and connect them with my calendar. Some people suggest that you should only read e-mail at certain times of the day; and that may work well for their jobs. However, I find I need to read e-mail throughout the day because I can then respond quickly to any time sensitive requests that may come up from faculty or other staff. I am constantly re-prioritizing and planning my daily tasks; that in itself takes time.

I use technology to some extent to help keep me updated with the latest professional news. I use RSS feeds (really simple syndication) on a "My Yahoo" page to keep up with law and library related blogs and news. I also get regular e-mail updates for publications like the *Chronicle of Higher Education* and news sources like CNN. I find this method to be a quick (but not necessarily in-depth) way to learn about news and trends that I might not have known about in the old days until I received them in a print newsletter or magazine.

My benchmarks are varied as well; if I am teaching, my primary benchmark is how well my students are learning the material, and if they seem to understand what I have been trying to teach them by the end of the course. My internal benchmarks in this area include my ability to grade papers on time; if my lecture was clear; and if I incorporated the latest information into my lectures and class syllabus.

Looking to the Future: Changing Areas of Library Science

There are so many ways in which library services are changing. I have a hard time thinking of any that will stay the same. Many are outside my area of expertise—for example, cataloging rules and metadata. However, I think they will be important with respect to how we control information, and how we get library patrons the information they are looking for in various formats. Due to the huge amount of online information available to the public and in the legal field, evaluating information in terms of quality is going to be an increasingly essential skill. Librarians are the most knowledgeable professionals to take the lead in this area and teach people how to evaluate information.

Final Thoughts

The key thing to keeping one's head clear in the midst of the changing requirements of a librarian's job is to keep your eye on the "target" of what you are trying to accomplish. For example, when our primary task is to enable our students to be skilled at research; we focus on getting them to know the basics of the research process and sources. After that basic structure is established within their minds, we can begin to add various new formats and methods. We always need to reevaluate our methods and consider whether they are improving our student's learning experience. Dealing with all of the different changes can be enjoyable if one remembers that the goals do not change, just the methods of how to reach them.

Barbara Glennan has worked in the library field since 1993. She is currently working as Assistant Director for Electronic and Outreach Services at California Western School of Law. Ms. Glennan received her J.D from Tulane University and a M. Libr. from the University of Washington.

Acknowledgment: *Thanks to Professor Phyllis Marion and Reference Librarian Brandon Baker for taking the time to review the text this chapter.*

Appendices

Appendix A: Law Firm Comments from My Legal Research Project   **150**

Appendix B: Sample Boot Camp Exercises & Answers   **154**

Appendix C: Online Research Task Survey   **157**

Appendix D: Research Task Book Survey   **158**

Appendix E: Print Must-Haves Survey   **159**

Appendix F: Pricing Plans   **160**

Appendix G: Law Firm Legal Research E-Questionnaire Results: Respondent Comments Regarding Excessive Research Costs   **162**

Appendix H: Introductory Class Exercise Examples   **166**

Appendix I: Sample Pre-Test/Post-Test Questions   **169**

Appendix J: Standards for Approval   **171**

Appendix K: Advanced Legal Research   **175**

Appendix L: Electronic Collection Development Policy Checklist   **178**

APPENDIX A

LAW FIRM COMMENTS FROM MY LEGAL
RESEARCH PROJECT

I have included only a portion of the comments in this appendix. Comments are edited for clarity by the use of bracketed text.

It is not so much that the techniques of legal research are unknown to them as it is the inability to analyze the substance of the law. The perfect course would combine legal research, analysis of the law, and legal writing. Finding the law, digesting the law, writing about the law as an integrated approach. It seems that the skills of researching the law, long associated with part of legal professionalism, are now considered something to be farmed out to others; i.e., librarians, law clerks, outsource attorneys. Partners seem to fear alienating new associates by making them do research. As one told me recently, that's not why they became lawyers.

It is tragic that the modern recent graduate does not appreciate the techniques of good legal research and writing. Good writing, supported by research, will insure partnership but youngsters do not seem to understand this. The thought process involved in good research is a skill which needs constant honing and contributes to overall good lawyering.

It just seems that the law school curriculum doesn't provide for enough opportunity for developing practical research skills. Even if they take legal research and advanced legal research, it won't really stick unless they have the opportunity to apply what they've learned.

It never fails to amuse me to go to AALL and watch lots of earnest academics talk about their devotion to legal research training. I don't know what you teach them but the net effect is pretty worthless. I would say only 10% of summers/first years have even a basic grasp of legal research. They are truly unprepared in every way. Skills seems to decline every year. It doesn't help that I have yet to meet an academic librarian who understood law firm economics or how contracts are billed. I would be happier with young associates who had never touched a computer in law school but could actually use a book.

It seems that they think they know everything... although sometimes they do know more than I do. However, I think it would be important that law clerks be taught how to use the print and online sources together. Sometimes, especially if it is a topic that I have never heard about, the print legal encyclopedias are a better way to start and then go online (i.e. Westlaw or LexisNexis) to get more information.

It usually takes the Summer Assoc. most of their stay with us to realize that we have treatises that discuss the problems they are researching.

It would be great if Westlaw and LexisNexis could print out the "street" cost of law students' searches so that they would be aware of the actual cost. We have "core competencies" questions that we give our Fall Associates. Then we review incorrect answers and at the same time show them their practice area research resources.

IT'S NOT ALL ONLINE!! Often, it's better to start your research in a print secondary source, where an expert in the field has probably already laid the groundwork for you. If you wish to try finding something on the Internet, place a strict time limit on your efforts (5-10 minutes, max). If you haven't found THE thing you're looking for, STOP and ask your friendly librarian. He or she will likely be able to take you right where you need to go, and your client won't be hit with a 2-hour bill for a 5-minute project.

It's hard to teach someone legal research. It's all about doing, so classes and seminars aren't necessarily the best way to go. However, trying to get an attorney to make an unbillable appointment and keep it is not an easy thing to do. I went through the same culture shock when I went from the classroom to the law firm library. I think the key is creating the relationships with the attorneys so we can take advantage of opportunities to teach and they can feel comfortable asking for help.

Law firm librarians, like myself, need to step up and do a better job of training our new associates regarding how [to] search in a cost-effective manner in online resources. We should not expect law schools to teach this. We also need to emphasize the importance of print materials.

Law school students come to law firms as either summer associates or fall associates without ever using the secondary sources in a law library. They have no, repeat *no* idea what a digest or jurisprudence is used for. They have never heard of Words and Phrases and do not know the value of looking at law review articles. Its been years since I had a summer or fall associate request Am Jur or Corpus Juris Secundum.

Law schools are doing a poor job of educating students in research, online or print. Online education is abdicated to company-provided trainers, who have little motivation to teach cost-effective training. Subject specific print training is ignored by professors. Librarians have no power to change the education system - it needs to come from the bar and the hiring firms. I'd love to see a research component added to the bar exam, but I know I won't live to see that day.

Law students are trained to use Westlaw/Lexis on a free basis - and so when they have to use it in the real world they have to re-learn how to search effectively.

Law students must be educated on what the real world costs are for CALR, and that, when in a firm setting, the client will likely be charged and that even a pro-rated dollar amount can be substantial. Also, despite what the CALR vendor says, future contract amounts WILL be based upon actual usage. Therefore, cost-effective techniques are essential skills.

Lecture them early, before they get into terrible habits; Give them the Lexis/Westlaw phone numbers - HIGHLY HIGHLY HIGHLY encourage that they use them, before logging on!

Legal research training in law firms is limited and has few incentives until the attorney runs up a large bill on Lexis or Westlaw. As for paper research, the new attorneys seem to have little or not experience with using them. They always go online or Google the question.

Let's blame it on the 6th grade teachers - research of any kind is not being taught from middle school on. The law schools are not to blame; but the law schools have to be the place when some intervention needs to be done. And we have to hear this from managing partners / hiring partners /

recruiters and not just the law firm and corporate and law school librarians. We've been screaming for many years.

Many attorneys start without knowing even the color of a state code book, much less how important it is. Many have no training in book research, so they can miss a lot of what is out there.

Many students don't realize the true costs of doing online research because it is free in school. I think they should take a course on costs of Lexis/Westlaw. I think there should be a greater emphasis on conducting cost effective research. I am concerned with flat rate contracts. While great for the firm in controlling costs, I believe it leads to bad habits in conducting legal research.

My concerns for legal research is that attorneys tend to forget how to use the print resources while they totally rely on Lexis and Westlaw systems. One must learn how to use the online resources as well as the print resources in order to become an efficient researcher. But with high real estate prices, the trend of having a traditional law library could be a thing of the past. Therefore, this would hurt the efficiency of legal research.

My main concern is that the newer attorneys don't know how to analyze the law. They are very literal in their searching. I think that someone should lead them to secondary treatises in their area, have them locate and read the primary laws and regs (online or off), then they can search in context. The lack of context is what I see as crucial. Also, determining what laws govern the question; ie, is it contract law, is it corporate law, is it [the] UCC?...the assigning lawyers often don't give the kids much guidance, and they flounder.

Courtesy of Patrick Meyer, Thomas Jefferson School of Law

APPENDIX B

SAMPLE BOOT CAMP EXERCISES & ANSWERS

Since we cover a lot of material in only two hours, these exercises need to be short as well as practical. These exercises were use specifically for our print research session.

CALIFORNIA RULES OF COURT:

Access *California Rules of Court. State.* Use the index to answer question a.

a. What California Rule of Court explicitly concerns the formatting of class action complaints?

Rule 3.761
[p. 693: Complaints – class actions; p. 692: Class actions – complaints]

b. Turn to the rule that you found for a. and tell me where the designation "CLASS ACTION" must appear on the complaint.

In the caption (first page, immediately below case number and above description of complaint)
[p. 110]

CALIFORNIA DIGESTS:

Answer the following questions using West's California Digest 2d.

a) Using the Descriptive Word Index, find an index cite regarding **a sentence for burglary being considered to be cruel and unusual punishment when it was similar in severity to the sentences of the principles** What is your **index cite AND** what is the **word path** used to find the cite (i.e., what primary word and subsequent words there under did you use to find your cite)? Your index cite should look something like this: **Sent & Pun k 123**

Cite: Sent & Pun k 1486
Path: Burglary – Sentencing & Punishment - Cruel or Unusual Punishment
[A-CI DWI, Vol 45, p. 487]

b. Look up your index cite from a) in the main volume. Cite to a case therein that was decided in 1984 and which held that **the active participant defendant's sentence for 25 years to life was not cruel or unusual**. Provide only the **case name**:

People v. Laboa
[v. 38C, p. 330]

Federal Court Documents:

Answer this question using *Matthew Bender Practice Guide. Federal Pretrial Civil Procedure in California.*

a) Find the index and then find a citation to a **sample Notice of Motion and Motion for Summary Judgmen**t. What is your index cite?

29.40
[index p. I-116: Summary Judgment – Sample Forms – Notice of motion and motion for summary judgment]

b) Look up your cite from a) in the appropriate main volume of this resource and write down the page number where the document appears:

p. 29-131

c) Start reading the document. In what court jurisdictions may you use this sample form?

Federal District Courts in California

Federal Forms:

a) Retrieve the index volume for *Nimmer on Copyright* and cite to a marketing agreement and software license form for the distribution of a computer program:

5: Form 27-5
[index vol. 11, p. I-20: Computer Programs – Forms – Marketing Agreement, software license &][forms – software (see computer programs0}

b) Look up the form from a). In what volume and on what page does the form start?

Vol 5, p. 27-24

Federal Forms:

a) Retrieve the general index volumes of *American Jurisprudence Legal Forms, Second Edition* and cite to a form for an advance payment (in money or cash) for a sale of goods:

§ 253:335
[L-Z index, p. 550: sales – payments – advance payments . . .]

b) Look up the form from a) in the appropriate *American Jurisprudence Legal Forms* main volume. In what volume and on what page does the form start?

v. 18, p. 293

Courtesy of Patrick Meyer, Thomas Jefferson School of Law

APPENDIX C

ONLINE RESEARCH TASK SURVEY

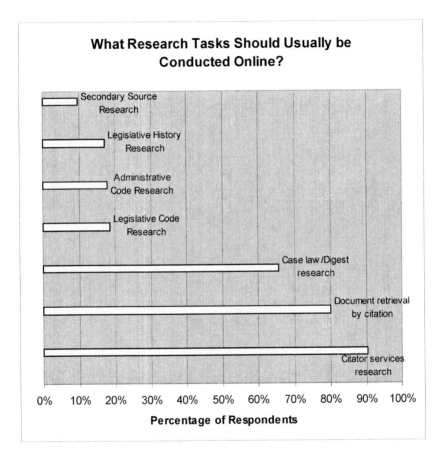

Courtesy of Patrick Meyer, Thomas Jefferson School of Law

APPENDIX D

RESEARCH TASK BOOK SURVEY

What Research Tasks Should Usually be Conducted in Books?

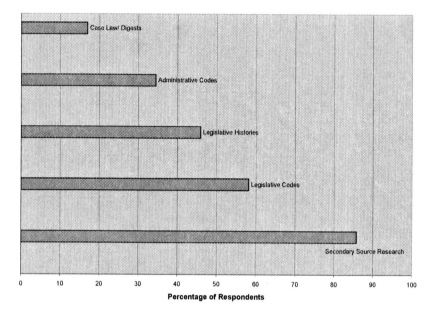

Courtesy of Patrick Meyer, Thomas Jefferson School of Law

APPENDIX E

PRINT MUST-HAVES SURVEY

What Print Resources Must New Attorneys Know How to Perform?

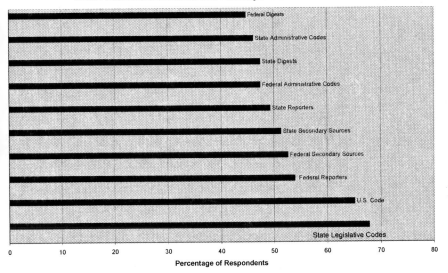

Courtesy of Patrick Meyer, Thomas Jefferson School of Law

APPENDIX F

PRICING PLANS

Westlaw

Have Flat Rate Plan	74%
Unlimited Flat Rate Plan	2.70%
Do Not Have Flat Rate Plan	22%
Have Transactional Plan	29.30%
Have Hourly Plan	25.30%
Do Not Subscribe to Westlaw	4.70%

LexisNexis

Have Flat Rate Plan	77%
Unlimited Flat Rate Plan	2.60%
Do Not Have Flat Rate Plan	19%
Have Transactional Plan	31.60%
Have Hourly Plan	23.00%
Do Not Subscribe to LexisNexis	3.90%

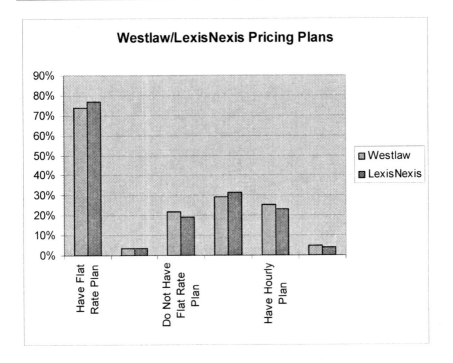

Courtesy of Patrick Meyer, Thomas Jefferson School of Law

APPENDIX G

LAW FIRM LEGAL RESEARCH E-QUESTIONNAIRE RESULTS: RESPONDENT COMMENTS REGARDING EXCESSIVE RESEARCH COSTS

These are some of the many comments to the question of "What are the reasons for excessive online research costs?" Comments are edited for clarity by the use of bracketed text.

Excessive usage out of the contract.

Unfamiliarity with the products and lack of experience in using the product.

-Reading cases while on [the] hourly [pricing plan]
-Changing databases and refining queries while on [the] transactional [plan]

1) Failure to use 'shortcuts' such as Get a Document, Focus/Locate, Book Browse, Table of Contents linking. 2) Use of hourly ID and spending hours online. 3) Printing many documents and using the Lexis or Westlaw print commands. 4) Going out of contract.

1) Ignorance of how flat-rate contracts work 2) Not using search language correctly 3) Moving too fast - hitting the search button without checking for spelling errors and then having to do the search again.

1) not understanding the question/issue. 2) unwilling to call Westlaw/Lexis and ask for help. 3) expecting the online source to be an oracle.

1) Unfamiliarity with how much Westlaw research actually costs 2) Inability to construct an effective search.

1) They think that they are still in law school and can use online [services] as long as possible 2) They have no idea on how to use print secondary sources to locate research and spend all of their time on the computer. 3) They are unprepared and inexperienced in using online databases effectively and efficiently 4) They do not understand basic research tools like digests, law reviews and restatements.

1. Inability to think through exactly what the correct method of researching any question might be. 2. Ignoring the print sources totally unless forced to think about them by partners. When I get a question I don't understand, if we have books, I read up a bit before I do an online search. Many times, I get the answer from the book without requiring online research at all. I wish I could say [that] I see associates doing this, but I can't. 3. No training or sensitivity to the actual costs incurred in researching online; unaware of the correlation between what they are doing on the PC and what shows up on the monthly statement in the client's bill.

1. Not understanding the difference between hourly and transactional [pricing plans]. 2. Staying online too long 3. Constructing searches that are too broad; not understanding Boolean.

1. Not logging off the web products but [instead just] closing the browser. 2. Confusion about hourly versus transactional IDs and when to use them. 3. Assuming that most research should start online and everything is available online. One individual downloaded an entire book and the cost was astronomical. 4. Ignorance about the high printing costs per document for news sources and other types of documents when attorneys want to "get everything."

Basically, they don't know where to begin, so they start with natural language searches of case law, find nothing specific, then frantically enter terms and read hundreds of cases online.

Choosing the wrong billing method; printing too many documents.

Clicking on links and not understanding how much they cost. Also, starting their research project by searching online first rather than using secondary source material. Using bigger databases than necessary. Not understanding the difference between hourly and transactional searching.

They do not have a command of the subject matter; Search strategy is not effective and they do not seek help; They do not have the ability to discern when a good print resource will provide a succinct yet effective answer.

Doing multiple searches instead of one broad search and then limiting or focusing the results. Looking in a large file or database instead of smaller ones.

Don't know the difference between hourly and transactional [pricing plans]; stay logged on to read through results; print off everything at ~$7+ per print.

Don't pay attention to training regarding cost-effective use of targeted research; don't call 1-800 numbers for assistance before embarking into unfamiliar territory; don't think to call the librarian to get ideas before going online.

Don't want to read the cases; don't know how to use the books (USCCAN, CFR) don't know the "bibles" treatises for given practice areas, haven't asked the billing partner, don't know how to limit databases (ALLFEDS vs. MO Cases); or a simple case of not reading book spines (Wright and Miller, Moore's Fed Practice, etc).

Either ignorance of cost billed to client or not keeping track of how they are performing the research.

Even though they come to a library orientation (usually a one-on-one experience) as part of their initial training, they forget that various databases which would incur no client charges are available to them. (Not sure that anything can be done about this) They forget how online searching is billed. Our IDs are mostly transactional (and they're told that) and many searches are done because they have not thought through beforehand as to what they should do. I feel that they're too comfortable doing what they could do in law school where there are no consequences.

Excessive case law research because 1) they do not know how to use the digest / key number features on Lexis and Westlaw 2) they do not know when to use transactional and when to use hourly billing.

Excessive printing; don't know how to differentiate between hourly and transactional search scenarios; using resources excluded from the contract; not being cost effective searchers.

Failing to do secondary research in treatises and practice guides (whether online or in print) before doing case research online (we do not have the print reporters). Using [the] hourly [pricing plan] when [the] transactional [plan] would be more appropriate.

Forming narrow searches and then re-running them rather than starting with a broad search and focusing. Not realizing that you pay for searches with zero results. Printing too much.

Getting caught up in the pressure of a task and thinking about getting the information without any thought as to the cost. Both getting the information and cost of that retrieval must be considered. Thinking or stating-"I learned Westlaw/Lexis in law school so I know how to research-I do not need additional training."

Going online immediately without first consulting primary or secondary legal materials in print to get a feel for the area of law; therefore reinventing the wheel when much of the research has been done in advance by editors and scholars.

Googling.

Googling and bad research skills in general; glazing over not paying attention to firm -- specific policies & information about our contacts and billing practices; lack of support for continued training from above although they complaint about the bills.

Have no understanding of the need / use of practice material, practitioner based research and resources. None at all. They always start in case law on Lexis or Westlaw, don't know how to do much else. Much to my dismay, discovered last year, many do not even really understand Boolean logic. Sigh.

Courtesy of Patrick Meyer, Thomas Jefferson School of Law

APPENDIX H

INTRODUCTORY CLASS EXERCISE EXAMPLES

These quick exercises are most effective if given shortly after the legislation, regulation or case law comes into being but before it appears in its normal place online. For instance, newly passed legislation does not automatically appear in a code set. Another example is that state trial court decisions are not on either Westlaw or LexisNexis. So basing a question on a state trial court case may be the basis for a good introductory exercise.

California Case Law: (3/31/08) 1) Using any means at your disposal, find the name and docket number of the recent California case concerning whether it is legal to drive a vehicle with one of the license plates not positioned in the normal upright position?; 2) What California law was in question in the case and how did the defendant violate the law?

Answers:
1) People v. Leonza Kevin Duncan, D050458
2) Cal Vehicle code § 5201; Front license plate was upside down, making it not clearly legible

Lesson:
Typical documents found via Google wouldn't have the docket number, so students will need to be savvy enough to either look for the official case law Website or to search in the correct Westlaw or LexisNexis databases. The wording of this scenario also helps students realize that the use of synonyms is a very important part of online research.

Federal Legislation: (2/11/08) President Bush signed a bill into law in December, 2007 that provided relief for thousands of people who were facing mortgage foreclosure. Use any source to find the title of the Act and its Public Law number. The public law number is often abbreviated at "PL".

Answer:
The Mortgage Forgiveness Debt Relief Act of 2007, P.L. 110-142

[sources: Thomas.loc.gov; Westlaw under US-PL; Lexis under USCS-Public Laws]

Lesson:
I used this example because at the time it had not yet been codified into the *U.S. Code*, as it is only updated periodically. You still have to know how to find new legislation – it's valid law but it's too new to be included in the *US Code*.

Federal Administrative Law: (2/28/08) In late January, 2008 the federal government announced the unveiling of a massive new database program that allows personnel to search several criminal identification databases what heretofore had to be searched separately, in order to strengthen anti-terrorist efforts. Using any desired means, find enough information on this program to provide me with the acronym for the program and its official *Federal Register* citation, which may be shown (abbreviated) as "FR".

ANSWER: (Federal Register database)
Acronym: ICEPIC
Cite(s):
73 FR 5460-01 (notice of proposed rule; 1/30/08)
73 FR 5577-03 (notice; 1/30/08)

Lesson: This would not be found yet in the *CFR*, which is a yearly codification of the *Federal Register*. They will not find the *Federal Register* citation from conducting their usual Google searches. The wording of this scenario also helps students realize that the use of synonyms is a very important part of online research.

Federal Administrative Law: (3/26/08) The Federal Energy Regulatory Commission submitted proposed rules the week of March 3rd, 2008 that are aimed at boosting competition in the wholesale electricity market as a way to keep consumer electricity costs down. You need to cite to the new proposed regulation in a court brief and you need its Federal Register citation. What is the *Federal Register* citation to this proposed rule?

Answer: (Federal Register database)
73 FR 12576-01

Lesson: This would not be found yet in the *CFR*, which is a yearly codification of the *Federal Register*. They will not find the *Federal Register* citation from conducting their usual Google searches. The wording of this scenario also helps students realize that the use of synonyms is a very important part of online research.

Courtesy of Patrick Meyer, Thomas Jefferson School of Law

APPENDIX I

SAMPLE PRE-TEST/POST-TEST QUESTIONS

My pre-test is administered on the first day of class and again (as the post-test) on one of the last days of class. It is currently comprised of 30 questions. Here are some sample questions:

Which is the official United States Code publication? (choose one):
USCA
USC
USCS

Which code set(s) provides annotations along with the actual text of the code sections? (choose all that apply)
USCA
USC
USCS

The legal rules and principals within each case are summarized at the beginning of cases in Westlaw. These summaries are called . . .
Casenotes
Footnotes
Headnotes

The popular Matthew Bender publications which include many California secondary source materials, are on which service? (Choose one)
Just Westlaw
Just LexisNexis
Both Westlaw & LexisNexis

Which official publication is a chronological compilation of federal statutes?
Code of Federal Regulations (CFR)
U.S. Statutes at Large
U.S. Code
Federal Register
I do not know

Give two examples of "Boolean" operators in either Westlaw or LexisNexis:

Give two examples of "proximity limiters" in either Westlaw or LexisNexis:

True or False: In LexisNexis, when you conduct an "edit search" you are searching within the documents that were just retrieved.

The popular Rutter Group materials, which include many California secondary source practice guides, are on which system? (Choose one)
Just Westlaw
Just LexisNexis
Both Westlaw & LexisNexis

The "Focus" function in LexisNexis allows you to (choose one)
Search through all of a chosen database
Search through already-retrieved documents
See if the original documents are still good law

Which of the following secondary legal sources contain citations to federal case law? (choose all that apply):
AmJur
US Supreme Court Reports
USCA
CFR
ALR Fed

True or False: It never costs money to use the "Locate in Result" function in Westlaw, or the "Focus" function in LexisNexis when using a flat rate or transactional pricing plan. (Choose one)
True
False
I do not know

Courtesy of Patrick Meyer, Thomas Jefferson School of Law

APPENDIX J

STANDARDS FOR APPROVAL

American Bar Association, Section on Legal Education and Admissions to the Bar, Standards for Approval of Law Schools (ABA: Chicago, IL 2007).

Standard 603. DIRECTOR OF THE LAW LIBRARY

(a) A law library shall be administered by a full-time director whose principal responsibility is the management of the law library.

(b) The selection and retention of the director of the law library shall be determined by the law school.

(c) A director of a law library should have a law degree and a degree in library or information science and shall have a sound knowledge of and experience in library administration.

(d) Except in extraordinary circumstances, a law library director shall hold a law faculty appointment with security of faculty position.

Interpretation 603-1
The director of the law library is responsible for all aspects of the management of the law library including budgeting, staff, collections, services and facilities.

Interpretation 603-2
The dean and faculty of the law school shall select the director of the law library.

Interpretation 603-3
The granting of faculty appointment to the director of the law library under this Standard normally is a tenure or tenure-track appointment. If a director is granted tenure, this tenure is not in the administrative position of director.

Interpretation 603-4
It is not a violation of Standard 603(a) for the director of the law library also to have other administrative or teaching responsibilities, provided sufficient resources and staff support are available to ensure effective management of library operations.

Association of American Law Schools, AALS Handbook, "Bylaws and Executive Committee Regulations Pertaining to the Requirements of Membership," (AALS: Washington, D.C. 2008).

http://www.aals.org/about_handbook_requirements.php

Executive Committee Regulations:

6-8.6   Staffing of the Library.

a.   The director of the library should have both legal and library education and should be a full participating member of the faculty.

b.   A member school shall have at least one professional librarian in attendance at all times when there is substantial use of the library.

Joint Statement on Faculty Status of College and University Librarians from the Association of College & Research Libraries.

http://www.ala.org/ala/acrl/acrlstandards/ALA_print_layout_1_192697_192697.cfm

Association of College and Research Libraries
Joint Statement on Faculty Status of College and University Librarians

Drafted by a committee of the Association of College and Research Libraries (ACRL), the Association of American Colleges (AAC), and the American Association of University Professors (AAUP). Approved by the membership of the Association of College and Research Libraries, a division of the American Library Association, June 26, 1972. Reprinted from the February 1974 issue of College & Research Libraries News, a publication of the Association of College and Research Libraries. Reaffirmed by the ACRL Board, June, 2001 and June, 2007.

As the primary means through which students and faculty gain access to the storehouse of organized knowledge, the college and university library performs a unique and indispensable function in the educational process. This function will grow in importance as students assume greater responsibility for their own intellectual and social development. Indeed, all members of the academic community are likely to become increasingly dependent on skilled professional guidance in the acquisition and use of library resources as the forms and numbers of these resources multiply, scholarly materials appear in more languages, bibliographical systems become more complicated, and library technology grows increasingly sophisticated. The librarian who provides such guidance plays a major role in the learning process.

The character and quality of an institution of higher learning are shaped in large measure by the nature of its library holdings and the ease and imagination with which those resources are made accessible to members of the academic community. Consequently, all members of the faculty should take an active interest in the operation and development of the library. Because the scope and character of library resources should be taken into account in such important academic decisions as curricular planning and faculty appointments, librarians should have a voice in the development of the institution's educational policy.

Librarians perform a teaching and research role inasmuch as they instruct students formally and informally and advise and assist faculty in their scholarly pursuits. Librarians are also themselves involved in the research function; many conduct research in their own professional interests and in the discharge of their duties.

Where the role of college and university librarians, as described in the preceding paragraphs, requires them to function essentially as part of the faculty, this functional identity should be recognized by granting of faculty status. Neither administrative responsibilities nor professional degrees, titles, or skills, per se, qualify members of the academic community for faculty status. The function of the librarian as participant in the processes of teaching and research is the essential criterion of faculty status.

College and university librarians share the professional concerns of faculty members. Academic freedom, for example, is indispensable to librarians, because they are trustees of knowledge with the responsibility of insuring the availability of information and ideas, no matter how controversial, so that teachers may freely teach and students may freely learn. Moreover, as members of the academic community, librarians should have latitude in the exercise of their professional judgment within the library, a share in shaping policy within the institution, and adequate opportunities for professional development and appropriate reward.

Faculty status entails for librarians the same rights and responsibilities as for other members of the faculty. They should have corresponding entitlement to rank, promotion, tenure, compensation, leaves, and research funds. They must go through the same process of evaluation and meet the same standards as other faculty members.[1]

On some campuses, adequate procedures for extending faculty status to librarians have already been worked out. These procedures vary from campus to campus because of institutional differences. In the development of such procedures, it is essential that the general faculty or its delegated agent determine the specific steps by which any professional position is to be accorded faculty rank and status. In any case, academic positions which are to be accorded faculty rank and status should be approved by the senate or the faculty at large before submission to the president and to the governing board for approval.

With respect to library governance, it is to be presumed that the governing board, the administrative officers, the library faculty, and representatives of the general faculty, will share in the determination of library policies that affect the general interests of the institution and its educational program. In matters of internal governance, the library will operate like other academic units with respect to decisions relating to appointments, promotions, tenure, and conditions of service.[2]

Notes

1. Cf. 1940 *Statement of Principles on Academic Freedom and Tenure*; 1958 *Statement on Procedural Standards in Faculty Dismissal Proceedings*; 1972 *Statement on Leaves of Absence*.
2. Cf. 1966 *Statement on Government of Colleges and Universities*, formulated by the American Council on Education, American Association of University Professors, and Association of Governing Boards of Universities and Colleges.

Courtesy of Barbara Bintliff, University of Colorado at Boulder

APPENDIX K

ADVANCED LEGAL RESEARCH

Instructor: Barbara Glennan	**Office Hours:** By Appt.
Class Time: Tuesday & Thursday: 10:50-12:05	**Office Telephone:**
Class Location: Multimedia Room 1B	**E-mail:**

Required Texts:

- **Where the Law Is: An Introduction to Advanced Legal Research, 2nd ed.,** Armstrong & Knott, Thomson/West, 2006
- **Basic Legal Research Workbook, *2nd ed.,*** Sloan & Schwinn, Aspen 2005
- **The Bluebook: A Uniform System of Citation, *18th ed.,*** 2005

Purpose:

Research skills are critical to the success of attorneys and law clerks. The goal of the ALR course is to provide all students who complete it the competence and confidence to confront their academic and professional legal research duties. Legal research is demanding and at times exasperating; knowing how to effectively approach and complete research on a legal issue will help ease some of its difficulty. Every student who puts serious effort into this course, (and receives a passing grade), can become a competent legal researcher.

Attendance:

Mandatory for all classes. CWSL requires that any student who misses more than 20% of the class sessions (which translates to 6) be dropped from the class with a grade of 51. It is suggested that classes not be unnecessarily skipped as allotted absences may be needed for emergency reasons. Material presented in class will be covered in the problems and quiz.

Readings:

Most of the readings will be from the class text. Supplemental readings are also required. These readings are from web sites, journal articles, and text chapters. Citations to these materials are listed below under the week they will be covered in class, or they will be announced in class. **Note: Students will save time and frustration by reading the assigned text <u>before</u> completing a related exercise.**

Grading:

Grades will be calculated based upon the completion of **legal research exercises (90%)** and one **quiz (10%).** According to California Western policy, the highest score that can be awarded is a 95. Final grades are based on a curve, and may not exactly match the raw score.

Exercises (85 points possible):

- There are 20 assignments throughout the semester. Some assignments will be handouts distributed in class. Most of the assignments are located in workbook.. These are divided into 15 separate problem sets: *Exercise A through Exercise O.* At the beginning of the semester, each student will be assigned a letter (A-O) and expected to complete that exercise set *__only__* for each assignment

- Assignments will be graded on a scale from **0 to 4.25.** If you score lower than **3.0**, you may re-do the assignment. You cannot score higher than a 3.0 on a redone assignment. **Re-dos must be completed within 2 weeks from the date the graded assignment is returned to you.**

- Assignments must be completed and submitted on time to receive full credit. There will be a penalty for late assignments. The highest possible score attainable will go down one point with each week the assignment is late. For example, if an assignment is one week late, the highest score you can attain will be a 3.25; two weeks late, 2.25. **If the assignment is more than 2 weeks late, you will __not__ receive credit for that assignment**. If there is a legitimate reason why you cannot complete the assignment on time, it is your responsibility to consult with one the instructor about your situation.

- Again, students will save time and frustration by reading the assigned text **before** completing a related exercise. Class lectures will contain highlights from the readings only. ___Students must do their own work on assignments___. **Assignments turned in that contain the same work (in the instructor's judgment) may be handed back as a redo for 1/2 or no credit**. Students are permitted to consult with classmates and/or the instructor for assistance in completing exercises, but are still required to go

9010

through the process of locating the information and answering the questions on their own.

- **Bluebook Format:** Bluebook citations will be required at some point in most of the exercises. The class will follow the court documents and legal memoranda format as described in the 'Bluepages'.

Quiz (10 points possible):

The quiz will be administered during the last class and consist of 10-20 multiple choice or short answer questions. It is 'closed book' and students will be allotted 30 minutes to complete it.

Courtesy of Barbara Glennan, California Western School of Law

APPENDIX L

ELECTRONIC COLLECTION DEVELOPMENT POLICY CHECKLIST

Name of Product: **Date of Evaluation:**
Publisher/Vendor & Contact Info:
Price:

Criteria	Comments	Initials
What format is the product provided in? • IP subscriptions to web based database, (preferred) • Password Access to web based database. • CD-ROM (not preferred)		
What are the licensing • IP access to all CWSL constituencies, including on campus use by walk in patrons. This is preferred. It is difficult to restrict otherwise. Other options: 1. Librarian mediated password? 2. Individual student/faculty passwords? • Can use resource for ILL? • Can we use resource for course packs?		

What information does the product provide? • Does it support our curriculum or faculty • Does it duplicate titles or materials already in the • Do we own or lease the information in this product?		
Who is providing the information? • Is the publisher known and credible? o Does the publisher have a track record of good customer support? • Is the author known and/or credible?		
Information quality: • Is the information provided updated at appropriate intervals? • Is the information provided accurate and credible? • Is access reliable, i.e. is the database often unavailable? • Is the information updated regularly?		

Interface: • Is the interface easily understandable to librarians and or patrons? • Is training provided by the vendor? • Is the library able to provide training if needed? • Is documentation provided?		
Pricing: • Is this the best price available to us? • Is there a one time cost or a recurring cost? • Are there hidden costs? • Is it available via consortia or has it been evaluated by a consortia?		
Cataloging: • Will it be cataloged? • If comprised of individual titles, will it be cataloged as a group or by individual title?		
Reviews: • Are there any published reviews of this resource? If so are they favorable?		
Purchase Product Y or N?		
Review at a later date?	Date:	
Not interested in product.		

Courtesy of Barbara Glennan, California Western School of Law

9010